The Best of the Berkshires

The Best of the Berkshires

Stephanie L. Johnson

The Globe Pequot Press

Old Chester Road
Chester, Connecticut 06412

Credit: Paul J. Rocheleau

THE BEST OF THE BERKSHIRES: This guide to country inns, restaurants and cultural gleanings has been written under no obligation to any commercal interest and has accepted no advertising.

The selections found herein are the author's own personal choice and description intended for the use of readers and may not be used for any other purpose without permission of the author and publisher.

Concentrated effort has been made to check and then double check listings, price ranges and hours. However, both are subject to seasonal change.

THANKS TO: Photographers Paul Rocheleau, Randy Trabold, Lewis C. Cuyler and Nicholas Noyes for their help and selected scenic photos. Also to the Berkshire Vacation Bureau of the Berkshire Hills Conference for permission to reprint the county map.

SPECIAL THANKS TO: Charles J. Bonenti for being a live-in editor, cheerleader, historian and four star at-home chef when the author ate out, or was too weary to eat in.

ABOUT THIS GUIDE: THE BEST OF THE BERKSHIRES, where to stay, eat, play, has been written from the selected personal choice of a year-round resident.

It is, we like to think, a careful, caring selection gleaned from the best of what the Massachusetts Berkshires offers. It stops clearly short of crossing the nearby borders into the Berkshire foothills of Connecticut, or venturing into the nearby New York Taconics and Vermont Green Mountains.

It would, alas, be too easy to add five more miles here, 10 more there, and diffuse the focus of what is closer at hand.

This guide is not a complete listing of everything the Berkshires has to offer. The quantity and scope of such an endeavor would fill a telephone directory and directories, we think, are not that much fun to read.

Activities change with the seasons, and your innkeeper can clue you in to what is happening on exactly the weekend you may randomly or selectively choose. Theaters and concerts offer advance seasonal schedules.

Nor is it a complete directory of all the places you might stay. Many perfectly fine, comfortable motels have been excluded in order to concentrate on the special experience you can only find in a charming New England country inn, or the special ambiance and atmosphere of a magnate's mansion now renovated and gone public.

Do not expect to find the biggest bargain, or the recommendation of an adequate, but not very memorable meal. Vacations are not times when you want mediocrity. They're special. And with the price of a good entree averaging about $8.50 we think you have every right to demand especially good, or interesting food, pleasant atmosphere and a memorable dining experience.

The author has made the assumption that if you drive two, maybe three or more, hours to come to see fall's spectacle of foliage, or brave the bristle of winter to ski across, or down, pristine white landscapes, or want to spend part of your summer laid back relaxing under tall pines under starlight skies listening to the Boston Symphony at Tanglewood, choose to fish here in our clear mountain streams, or hike in numerous state forests, you have a discerning taste for the best in New England life. We think the "Beautiful Berkshires'" offers it.

In two months this writer has eaten extensively in over 30 restaurants not previously tried, and lost weight in the process.

"That," laughed one congenial innkeeper, "doesn't seem to say

Credit: Randy Trabold

much for our food."

She was, in fact, quite wrong. It is a superb testimonial to how fast you have to run to take in the culinary and cultural offerings found in these hills. Not all of it is, of course, exceptional, but much of it is unusually good. We have been picky in choosing.

The Berkshires, as you'll discover, have a rich heritage and interesting history that has already filled and inspired many volumes, enticed many artists.

Its natural and man-made offerings appeal with equal ardor to naturalist, tourist, scholar, musician, painter, writer, sportsman, citizens of the weary world, or frenzied city sophisticate alike.

Welcome to this relaxing, worldlywise place where nature mostly still visibly has her way.

You can't see and do everything that is here in a weekend, or even really gulp it all down in a summer.

Pick a little at a time and take your time. The Berkshires have been around a long time. Change here does not happen fast.

You'll probably find yourself coming back again and again.

Every year thousands of old faithfuls bounce back to the Berkshires, and every year countless newcomers are bitten by the Berkshire bug.

We were. And one summer never left.

A word about prices mentioned in this guide. As the seasons change so do the prices. Mostly, they go up. Listings are intended to give you a range or average to judge by. Use them as a guidepost and factor in inflation as a continuous fact of life.

October

CONTENTS

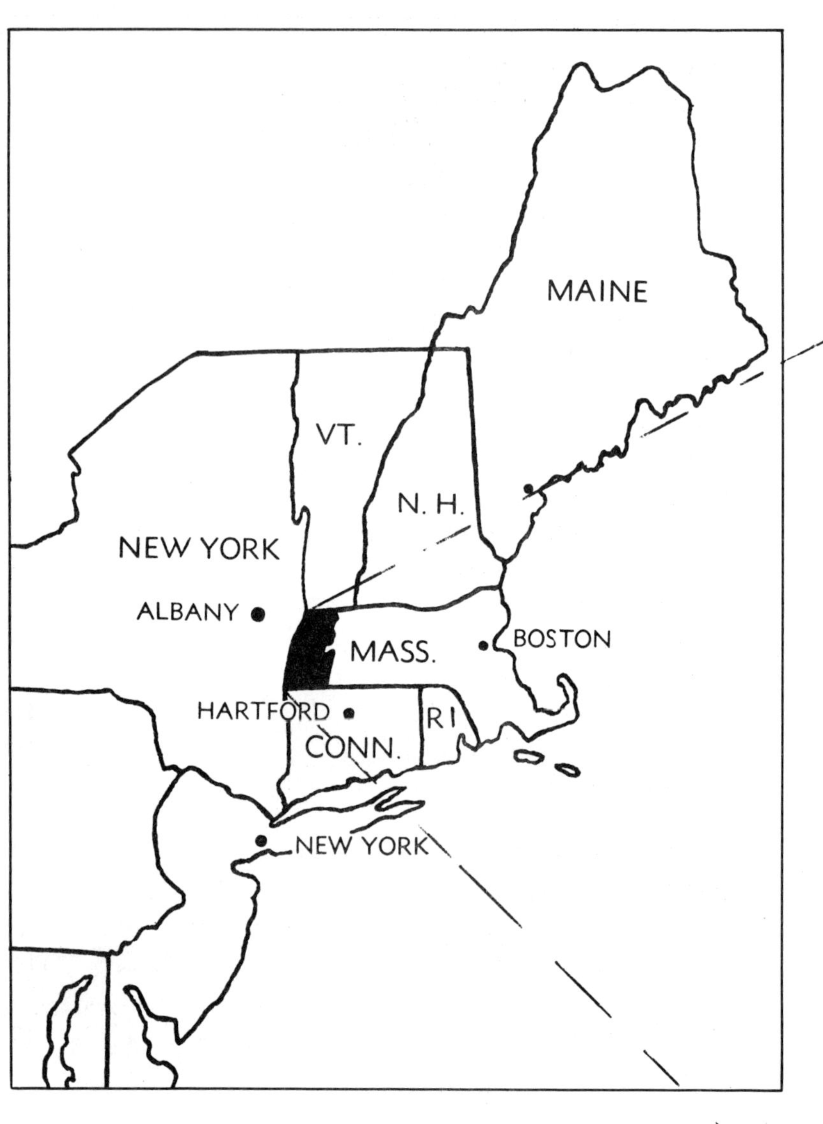

MAINE
VT.
N. H.
NEW YORK
ALBANY
MASS.
BOSTON
HARTFORD
R I
CONN.
NEW YORK

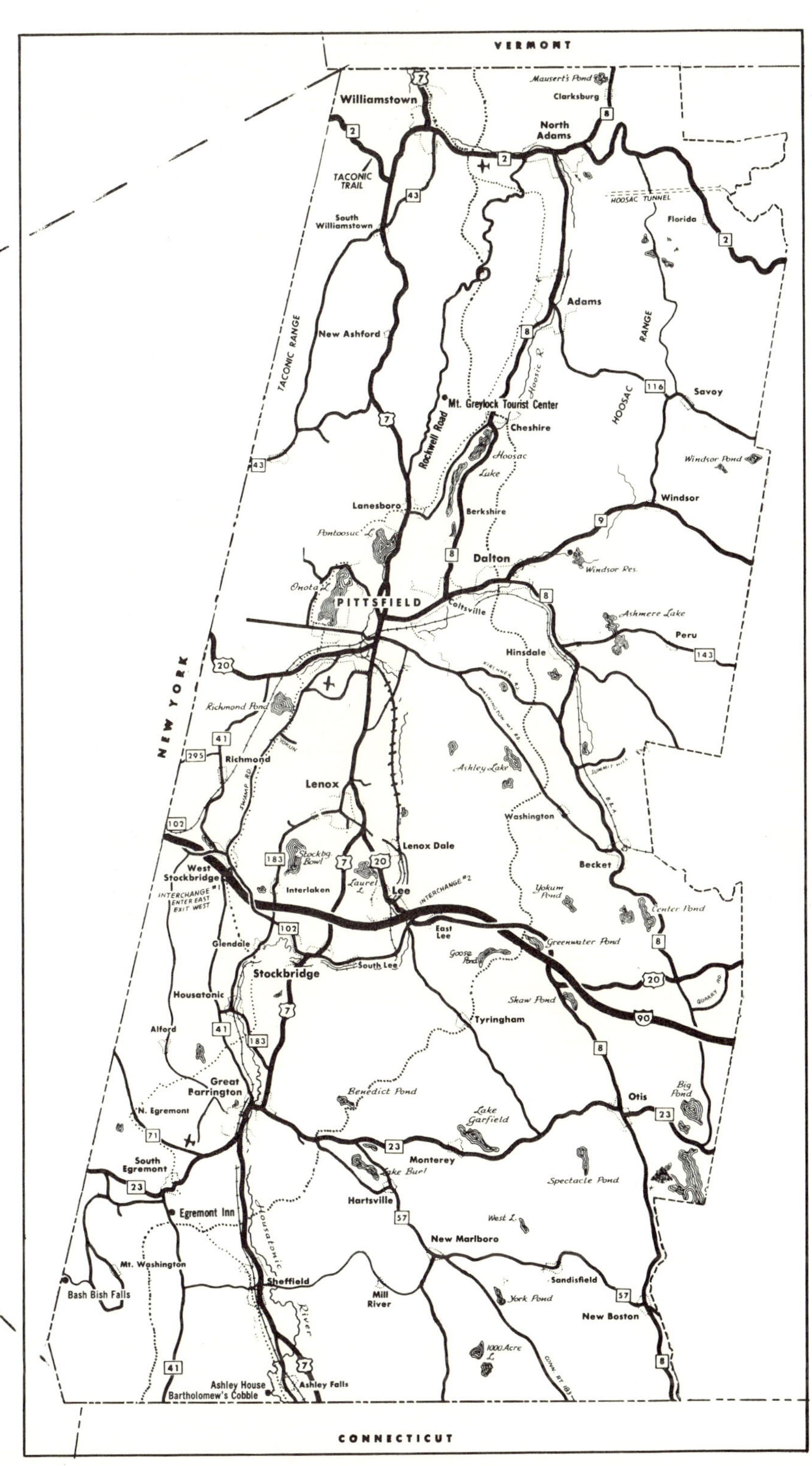

VERMONT
NEW YORK
CONNECTICUT
Williamstown
TACONIC TRAIL
South Williamstown
New Ashford
TACONIC RANGE
Mt. Greylock Tourist Center
Rockwell Road
Lanesboro
Pontoosuc L.
Onota L.
PITTSFIELD
Cheshire
Hoosac Lake
Berkshire
Coltsville
Mausert's Pond
Clarksburg
North Adams
Adams
Hoosic R.
HOOSAC RANGE
HOOSAC TUNNEL
Florida
Savoy
Windsor Pond
Windsor
Windsor Res.
Dalton
Hinsdale
Ashmere Lake
Peru
Richmond Pond
Richmond
SWAMP RD.
YOKUN
Lenox
Ashley Lake
KIRCHNER RD.
WASHINGTON MT. RD.
SUMMIT HILL
B & A
Washington
Lenox Dale
Stockbg. Bowl
Interlaken
Laurel L.
Lee
INTERCHANGE #2
Becket
Yokum Pond
Center Pond
West Stockbridge
INTERCHANGE #1
ENTER EAST
EXIT WEST
Glendale
East Lee
South Lee
Goose Pond
Greenwater Pond
QUARRY RD.
Stockbridge
Housatonic
Shaw Pond
Tyringham
Alford
Great Barrington
Benedict Pond
Lake Garfield
Otis
Big Pond
N. Egremont
South Egremont
Egremont Inn
Housatonic River
Lake Buel
Hartsville
Monterey
Spectacle Pond
West L.
New Marlboro
Mt. Washington
Bash Bish Falls
Sheffield
Mill River
York Pond
Sandisfield
New Boston
CONN. RT. 181
1000 Acre L.
Ashley House
Bartholomew's Cobble
Ashley Falls

Credit: Paul J. Rocheleau

1. THE BERKSHIRES

A GLANCE BACK IN TIME

The story of the Berkshires is really the story of all New England, wrested from the Indians, cleared and farmed, molded by changes in the national economy into an industrial belt and finally a leisure environment.

The Berkshires were a wilderness, inhabited by Indians when the first white settlers pushed into the Housatonic River Valley in the 1720s and started to clear the land for farming. By 1800, the Indians had been driven out, the land cleared at such a pace that by 1820 even the mountains had been stripped bare of trees to make way for pastures and fields.

Farming has never been easy in New England. The growing season is short and the land too hilly and rocky for efficient cultivation. As new areas opened for settlement in the Ohio River Valley, many Berkshire farmers abandoned their homesteads here and moved west.

By then, however, the water-powered textile loom had been invented and was coming into use. New England was land poor, but it had fast-running streams in abundance and mills began to sprout everywhere, boosting the prosperity and brightening the future of Berkshire towns like Pittsfield, Adams, North Adams and Lee.

The abandoned farmsteads were slowly reclaimed by forests that created gentle patterns of growth and clearing among the rock walls and winding roads. The Berkshires took on a quiet, pastoral quality that attracted, first, artists and writers, and then new millionaires, with their industrial fortunes, time and leisure.

The Berkshires, particularly around Lenox and Stockbridge which were easily accessible to New York and Boston, became a kind of rich man's country preserve, checkered with vast estates built to resemble English manor houses.

Taxes, wars, and depressions in the 20th century ended that kind of lavish lifestyle forever and by mid-century many of the county's paper and textile mills had folded as well, victims of a shift in industry to the Sun Belt states.

Now, the Berkshire economy has shifted to tap a new resource, the thousands of visitors who come here each year, with cars and leisure time, to ski, to enjoy the wealth of music, dance and summer stock and to taste the quiet, gentle rural landscape woven with 250 years of human history.

Ask someone who lives here what the Berkshires are like and you are just as likely to be asked, "Which part?"

The Berkshires are mountains, trees, Tanglewood, of course, but also tiny farm villages frozen in time, old mill towns that have seen better days, small cities and suburbs, and uplands where trappers still lay their lines. The landscape is a little bit of everything.

There is no range of mountains here called "The Berkshires," despite what many people think. Berkshire means simply "the forest shire," and refers to the region roughly outlined by what is marked off as Berkshire County.

The mountain ranges are Taconic bordering New York State, and the Hoosac, rising in the east and separating the county from the rest of Massachusetts. In between lies the broad Housatonic River valley whose river flows through Connecticut to Long Island Sound. Another narrow valley, carved by the Hoosic River which empties into the Hudson, slashes across the county in the north.

This pattern of mountains and valleys, created by four advances of glaciers, the last one 10,000 years ago, separates the Berkshires into distinct regions, each with a character and lifestyle of its own.

If you're pining for classic New England towns with white churches and village greens, take Route 23 and Route 57 through South County. This is historic farm country and many of the communities you'll pass — Egremont, Monterey, New Marlborough and Sandisfield — still look pretty much as they probably did 200 years ago. Great Barrington is the commercial hub of activity here.

South County has become a smart and expensive place to live, drawing executives, writers and theater people from New York and Fairfield County which is one to two hours south.

If the good life appeals to you, go to Stockbridge and Lenox, fashionable playgrounds of the rich in the 19th century and still "the place" to be seen here in the summer. Most of the big manor houses have been turned into private schools or inns, but the surroundings are still lush and stately, the restaurants among the best and most expensive around, and the shops filled with casually chic sportswear, crafts, and gourmet goodies. Here you'll find Tanglewood, summer home of the Boston Symphony Orchestra, also the Berkshire Theatre, the most after dark nightlife, dancing

and maybe a celebrity or two. The crowd is smart and sophisticated. The best place to watch it is the porch or back garden of the Red Lion Inn. Sooner or later everyone stops in here.

If you're interested in mill towns and bargains at factory outlets, take Route 8 north from Pittsfield through Adams and North Adams, both former textile and papermaking communities. Nowadays you'll see 19th century brick mills, the ornate mansions their owners lived in and the simple tenements and row houses that were inhabited by the mill hands.

Several of the mills have outlets for fabric and wallpapers like Schumacher and Grieff, and sporting goods. The Windsor Mill in North Adams has been turned into working space for craftsmen.

If you are a wilderness lover, take Route 2 west from North

Adams into the mountains of Florida where you'll find deep forests, dramatic views, icy streams and air that's cool and fresh in the dead heat of any summer. Be sure to drive to the top of Mt. Greylock in Adams, or hike up Monument Mountain in Great Barrington when you're in south county to see the county spread beneath you like a patchwork quilt. While you're in the north, amble on up the Mohawk Trail, stopping at Hairpin Turn and ending at Whitcomb Summit.

If you want to see our idea of the ideal New England college town, stop off in Williamstown, home of Williams College, set back on expansive lawns against fine old elm trees. Ivy-covered campus buildings in multiple architectural styles as well as handsome colonial and Victorian houses dot the landscape. One of the prettiest rural drives is along or above Green River Road. Be sure to see the Clark Art Institute if you are an art lover. It boasts one of the country's finest collections of Impressionists paintings. Also for 25 years this town has been the home of the Williamstown Summer Theatre Festival now nationally known for the quality of its productions and guest stars.

Pittsfield, the county's major city and home of its biggest employer, the General Electric Co., is the financial and retail hub of the central Berkshires and boasts an historic center, Park Square, that's on the National Register of Historic Places. It also has the largest variety of shops priced from five and dime to Gucci-like tastes, and the largest area hotel, a Hilton. Just outside of Pittsfield from the city line to Lenox along Route 7 are more motels and motor inns than you can count on two hands.

The Berkshires, then, are not unlike the patchwork quilts you may find in local church bazaars and antique shops. You can select any patch, look again, and always see something a little bit different.

WHEN TO COME

If you like your scenery spiced with the maximum of cultural offerings summertime is the prime time to come.

Tanglewood swings into gear July 1, The Berkshire Theatre in Stockbridge and the Williamstown Theatre Festival in Williamstown pop their season champagne corks around the end of June. Dance kicks up its heels at Jacobs Pillow in Becket, and there's usually more to do than time to do it in.

They all roll up their seasonal tents, pack it all in at the end of August and there is a noticeable lull from pre-Labor Day through mid- September. South county towns, particularly Lenox and Stockbridge, quiet down and appear to roll up the sidewalks. Some of the inns and restaurants in Lenox's "restaurant row" take a break and close kitchens for a week or two.

The lull is short lived. Around the end of September through the first two weeks of October things start to pick up again as fall nips the air and fall's foliage turns a spectacular hue.

At the height of this season, which usually peaks somewhere

near Columbus Day weekend, give or take a week in either direction, the leaf peeper's Connecticut, Vermont, New York, New Jersey, and even Ohio license plates are commonplace and bumper to bumper. Lodging is booked in some places seasons ahead, restaurants are crowded, reservations well in advance are a *must.*

It's not a time to decide to amble up here unprepared with no idea where to stay unless you're free spirited enough not to mind flying off a distance to find a place with a rare vacancy sign.

From late October to Thanksgiving the influx of activity quiets down again. But then the idea of an old fashioned Thanksgiving in a quaint New England town and visions of Norman Rockwell's family type gatherings bring back weekenders to second homes and inns which perk up and put their best dressed turkeys and hams forward.

Sometimes as early as Thanksgiving the snow flies and a winter world awaits skiiers who crowd in for increasingly popular and unpopulated cross country skiing or down hill skiing at nearby Bousquet, Brodie, Butternut Basin, Otis Ridge, Catamount and Jiminy Peak. Skiing can last as long as Easter if they are lucky, and the snow stays.

Winter is not a gentle time. Temperatures can drop early morning and late night to minus 10 or minus 20, but mostly they hover around the low thirties during the day. Locals are accustomed to dealing with snow and ice since winter is the longest season, and the town highway crews are out before dawn clearing the roads and main thorough fares. It's not uncommon once or twice a season for skiiers to be snowed in up here unable to make it down a clogged Taconic, Mass Pike, or New York Thruway, but able easily to make it to the local slopes. Weekends like that they pray for, particularly around Washington's birthday.

Spring is rather short and often missed. It follows quickly on the sticky heels of the fifth season known hereabouts as "mud season." The buds on the trees, apple blossoms, and daffodils in the gardens are about two weeks behind their southern New York or metropolitan Boston counterparts, and a chill still nips the Berkshire air. Trees go from fuzzy to full blown so quickly many think it happens overnight when they are sleeping. Spring is more readily visible in the advance warning rush of melting brooks swollen with run off from the mountains, the melting of ice and soft mushy ground.

Wary gardeners hold off most of their planting outdoors until Memorial Day weekend for fear of a late frost which gives you

some idea of nature's mecurical whim.

Back full circle to summer, Berkshire summers are exhuberant. Berkshire means forest shire and the forests, valleys, and gently green carpeted hills become a veritable Green Mansions. Although temperatures can soar to the high nineties, city mugginess is short lived and infrequent. The air is not polluted. Nights are almost always cool. Carrying a sweater or shawl to a late concert or theatre is considered to be common sense rather than caution.

WHAT TO WEAR

The Berkshires are populated by country towns surrounded by overlapping mountain ranges. But before you think people here dress like home on the range, early Appalachia, or L. L. Bean, pause a moment in packing.

The Berkshires have been a fashionable summer place for 200 years. Lenox in its heyday from about 1880 to World War I was one of the richest little towns in the nation. The "inland Newport" it was called.

Williamstown has been a college town since 1793.

And in recent years the Berkshires has become increasingly popular with contemporary craftsmen.

Added up it makes for an interesting eclectic, if not terribly au courant, fashion portrait.

Everyone, it seems, subscribes to the guideline: dash, but not flash when it comes to clothing.

Far out trends, way down cleavages and sparkle plenty get a look, usually of surprise.

New Englanders of means aren't ostentatious about flaunting it. It's almost as though they grew up with the inbred notion that, as one chronicler of the passing parade put it, "one should never look as though one tried too hard."

There's still a look of old school tweeds, an understated nonchalance and a suburban weekend sportswear approach during the week.

Berkshire residents seem conservative and somewhat restrained in appearance. But it is not a stuffy place. Properly dressed in the opinion of one top restaurant "doesn't necessarily mean a jacket and tie, but simply neat and tidy, sophisticated."

The older set interprets this by blazers and green, red and plaid sports jackets which bloom at the summer theaters and Tanglewood. But if you want to forego the jacket in favor of polo shirt and sports slacks no one looks askance.

Older women favor long summer skirts, sun dresses, or smart slacks and tops for evening.

The younger crowd subscribes to the "anything goes" tune. But bare or sandal footed, jean clad diners are likely to be told gently, but not rudely, "we don't think you'd be comfortable in the dining room like that." At least that's the way one south county "better restaurant" handles their aversion to a dress code.

Picnickers on Tanglewood's lawn are another matter. They have been known to wear and bring anything from jeans and a hunk of baloney to long dress, pate and champagne. Tanglewood has elevated picnicking to a high art.

Backpackers, campers or hikers we've left out. They have their own dictates.

As for the rest of us, casual, comfortable, in good taste are the fashion passwords, keeping in mind that this is, after all, New England where restraint is something of a habit.

Appearance aside, New Englanders are warm and friendly, helpful and approachable. They come through when you need them, and the rest of the time figure they'll just go about their own affairs and mind their own business.

If they turn their heads to look at out of towners they either look good or odd. If you don't know the difference they are not likely to worry about it, probably neither should you.

HOW TO GET HERE

Berkshire County is three hours from New York City as the crow flies, if it doesn't stop along the way. Also three hours from Boston, one hour from Albany, two hours from Hartford, Connecticut.

If you actually do fly, Command Airways serving Pittsfield and the Berkshires, has four flights daily, two from Kennedy and two from La Guardia.

Pittsfield is 37 miles from Albany Airport, 70 from Bradley

Field, Connecticut.

Charter service from North Adams, Pittsfield and Great Barrington airports is also possible.

By bus the Berkshires can be reached from Albany, Hartford, and New Haven via the Arrow Line into Pittsfield.

Vermont Transit services Pittsfield from New York.

Bonanza will get you from Providence, R.I., Springfield, Mass., Albany, N.Y. and Boston to North Adams, Pittsfield and Williamstown. Greyhound Lines from Boston and New York arrive in Williamstown, nearby Bennington Vt., and Pittsfield.

Amtrak trains arrive at Albany Rensselaer Station from Boston, New York and Chicago, and at Pittsfield from Boston and Chicago.

By car, coming from New York, take the Taconic Parkway to the Massachusetts Turnpike. Lee is Exit 2, Lenox is reached via Route 20 north, Stockbridge, Route 102 west, Pittsfield, Route 7 north merges with Route 20 in Lenox, Williamstown via Route 7 north.

From Connecticut take the Connecticut Turnpike to Route 91 north which intersects with the Massachusetts Turnpike then follow the above directions.

From New Jersey take the Garden State Parkway to the Gov. Thomas E. Dewey Thruway. At Massachusetts Turnpike exit follow the above directions.

From Boston take the Mass Turnpike and get off at Exit 2, Lee.

For additional travel information phone or write: Berkshire Hills Conference, Inc., 20 Elm St., Pittsfield, Massachusetts 01201, 413-443-9186.

HELPFUL INFORMATION SOURCES

There are nine county information booths, most open only in summer, where tourists can load up on pamphlets, peruse nearby restaurant menus, ask for reservation help, or just plain directions. Town pamphlets indicating interesting walking tours and points of interest are also available for the asking.

In north county, information booths may be found at: Williamstown, corner of Main and North Streets, Route 2, open daily July and August, weekends until October. In North Adams, the Northern Berkshire Chamber of Commerce at 69 Main Street is open all year round, booths are at 1 Main Street, Mohawk Center and 121 Union Street, Route 2, the latter open only in summer.

In south county the Lenox Chamber of Commerce maintains a booth July and August in the Academy Building on Main Street.

In Lee, a booth is located at Route 20, corner of the Park, open July and August, fall weekends.

In Stockbridge, their booth is on Main Street, and is open July and August.

In south county, Great Barrington Chamber of Commerce maintains a booth all year round at 362 Main Street (Route 7).

Just off the Massachusetts Turnpike at the Howard Johnson's in Lee is a year round information booth.

Winter skiiers seeking toll free checks on conditions and needing information from *outside the state* may call: 800-628-5030.

Inside Massachusetts call 413-499-0700.

New England Ski Council reports are broadcast twice daily, Tuesday through Saturday, from radio station WBEC AM, Pittsfield.

The major newspapers serving Berkshire county daily are The North Adams Transcript circulating in north county, and the Berkshire Eagle serving south, central and north county.

Both papers publish free summer magazines bi-weekly and weekly which list calendars of local events, features of interest and nearby over-the-border attractions. The Transcript publishes SummerScope beginning June 30 every two weeks until the end of August. The Eagle publishes Berkshire Week weekly through summer, and Upcountry, a regional New England magazine in tabloid form, every month year round.

In summer the Berkshire Vacation Bureau has three county numbers toll free for daily events. The numbers change yearly, but are well publicized.

Credit: Paul J. Rocheleau

COUNTRY INNS

Candlelight Inn

Address:	53 Walker Street, Lenox, Mass., 01240, 413-637-1555
Innkeeper:	James De Mayo
Rooms:	6 with double bed occupancy and bath
Rates:	$35 off season, $45 summer double occupancy
Facilities:	Center of Lenox location, restaurant. Al fresco dining.

The summer of 1978 was the first season under James De Mayo's ownership, management and hand in the kitchen.

The rooms are spacious, brass beds, marble top dressers, Colonial wallpapers.

The food here is excellent. Mr. De Mayo believes in "cooking from the old school" meaning vegetables are fresh, they bone their own veal and chicken, make homemade soups daily.

(See restaurants for details.)

The inn is dead center of Lenox, a hop-skip to Tanglewood, Berkshire Theatre in Stockbridge, within walking distance of Lenox shops.

Cross country skiing in winter at the town's Kennedy Park and at nearby Pleasant Valley Wildlife Sanctuary. Rentals can be had from the Arcadian Shop in town.

Dalton House

Address:	955 Main Street, Dalton, Mass., 01226, 413-684-3854
Innkeepers:	Gary and Bernice Turetsky
Rooms:	Six doubles
Rates:	$30 per couple, summer; $22, winter. Includes breakfast.
Facilities:	Dining room, breakfast only; living room with fireplace and loft lounging area.

The Dalton House has the kind of cozy, congenial atmosphere that invites you to sit down, take off your shoes and unwind in front of the fire over mugs of hot coffee or cider. And if it feels like you're in someone's living room, rather than a public inn, that's just the way innkeepers Gary and Bernice Turetsky planned it. They live here too, in the main house. The greenhouse and flower shop next door they also own and run.

Relative newcomers to the Berkshires, they opened the Dalton House early in 1978 in what had been a private residence, built in 1810 by a Hessian soldier. Four of the guest rooms and the dining and living rooms are in a new wing, built in a colonial style, and two are in the main house. All the rooms are furnished in an early American style and have either private or adjoining modern baths. The two rooms in the main house we found the most charming with antique moldings and fireplaces.

The Turetskys do not serve full meals, nor is there a bar, but guests may sit down at the dining room table in the morning and help themselves to fruit, cheese, a variety of muffins and coffee, all included in the price of the room.

Egremont Inn

Address:	South Egremont, Mass. 01258, 413-528-2111
Innkeepers:	Robin and Rudyard Propst
Rooms:	23 rooms, private baths, air conditioning
Rates:	$30-$45 double occupancy weekends summer; $25-35, off season, does not include meals. Two day minimum summer and fall. Three day minimum holiday weekends. Breakfast, lunch and dinner. Bar. Closed three weeks in November.
Facilities:	Tennis courts, swimming pool, cross country skiing here and certified instruction. Golf nearby.

Once a coach stop for passengers heading west to Albany, or east over the mountains to Boston, the inn was built by Francis Hare and hired help from his neighbors back in 1780. Finished just in time for Christmas, the glow of its candles and firesides have lit a welcome to travelers ever since.

Wide planked floors, beamed ceilings, antiques, hooked rugs and wooden bowls filled with polished apples await you in the fall.

The inn's bedrooms are casually comfortable, happily without telephones or televisions.

The dinner menu leans conservatively toward the safe side with half a dozen selections such as veal, chicken, pork chops, steak and lamb entrees averaging $9.50. The light menu affords a wider selection of more modestly priced offerings like a pate plate with homemade breads, $3; assorted cold sausage plate, $3.50; omelettes, salads, sandwiches and burgers, $2.50 average.

Their vegetables are fresh, salads are mixed greens instead of bland iceberg, homemade soups like cream of carrot are very good.

Desserts include Victorian orange cake, $1.75, carrot cake with strawberry filling and German chocolate cake, $1.75.

The porch in summer is a delightful place to sit and sip.

In winter marked cross country trails behind the inn are a good place for beginners to get their balance. Certified instructors and ski rentals at the inn will get you off on the right foot to start.

A hop-skip from the Connecticut border, here in the southwest corner of the state you are away from the hustle bustle of south county traffic, yet still within a half hour of south county attractions.

Fairfield Inn

Address:	Route 23, Great Barrington, Mass. 01230, 413-528-2720
Innkeeper:	Joan Shoreman
Rooms:	11 with bath, air conditioning. Closed Tuesday. Breakfast, lunch, dinner. Bar.
Rates:	$28-$38
Facilities:	Three miles west of center of Great Barrington, across the street from the Egremont Golf Club. Swimming pool, cross country skiing in winter.

A cosy comfortable rambling inn, the Fairfield Inn can accommodate 25 guests. A homey atmosphere greets you when you walk in the door past the bar to a lounge that nestles around a fireplace. The dining room to the right is a pleasant room curtained with Austrian shades.

Each bedroom upstairs is different, scattered with collected antiques, and some canopy beds.

Outside porches and terrace dining in summer are shaded with age-old oaks and maples. Sloping lawns lead to a pond inhabited by ducks.

The menu here leans to continental and American dishes, fresh fish such as the poached Nova Scotia salmon with hollandaise at $8.95 is quite good.

There is also brook trout almondine, Dover Sole in lemon butter, fresh bay scallops mornay or broiled in sherry, frog legs provencal and lobster. Prices for entrees average $9.95.

Meat lovers will find prime ribs with Yorkshire Pudding, $10.95, tournedos with bernaise, lamb chops, three kinds of veal, duckling with wild rice.

Homemade soups and breads, fresh vegetables and home baked pies and cakes.

Wines have been chosen from the Pedroncelli Winery in California's Sonoma County.

Mrs. Shoreman, who runs the inn, was born to the business. Seven generations of her family have been involved in pubs. In England they are even licensed as Publicans, which means given a license to serve the public.

Especially popular with older golfers, the inn is just about within teeing distance of the Egremont Country Club where guests can golf in summer, cross country ski in winter.

Flying Cloud Inn

Address:	South Sandisfield Road, Route 57, New Marlboro, Mass., 01230, 413-229-2113
Innkeepers:	Robert and Diane Rolfs
Rooms:	9 guest rooms, most private bath, two share
Rates:	$39-$45 per person weekends, includes two meals, gratuities, tennis, cross country skiing; weekdays, $36-$41 per person. Minimum two night stay, three on holiday weekends.
Facilities:	Two tennis courts, swimming in spring fed, trout stocked pond, cross country skiing in winter, snow shoeing, sleds and toboggans, equipment on premises, summer lawn games, four miles walking trails.

Everybody raves about this charming pure New England inn situated in the middle of nowhere, but from which it's still possible to get somewhere like Tanglewood in half an hour.

Named after a famous American clipper ship, the inn is a remodeled white clapboard farmhouse with nine guest rooms, room for 20 guests.

A veritable colonial retreat from the bustle of summer in Stockbridge, the Flying Cloud nestles in a bucolic setting amid 20 acres of lawns, meadows, woods and glens.

The guest rooms are a medley of patchwork, flocked wallpaper and grandfather clocks. The food is hearty New England and continental with fresh garden vegetables. Buffet style breakfast may include ham, pancakes, chicken livers, homemade breads and rolls. Meals are served only to house guests.

Excellent wine cellar.

Reserve a berth in this country ship well in advance, space flies here.

The Red Lion Inn

Address:	Route 102, Stockbridge, Mass. 01262, 413-298-5545
Innkeepers:	Owned and operated by Senator and Mrs. John H. Fitzpatrick. Betsey M. Holtzinger, innkeeper.
Rooms:	100 with or without bath
Rates:	Rates vary widely depending on season, size of room, bath. A summer season double with private bath is $48; with shared bath, $36. The inn closes beginning of November for two weeks, reopens for Thanksgiving.
Facilities:	Center of town location, near to all major south county attractions, this being one of them

The Red Lion sits like a fat old white cat purring contentedly at the corner of Stockbridge.

Standing foresquare and elegant, a landmark at Main and

South Streets, it has been an inn in one way or another since 1773 when it was just a stagecoach stop on the Albany to Boston route.

Senator and Mrs. Fitzpatrick bought it in 1968 and have operated it since as the grand old lady of colonial inns restoring and refurbishing the inside and out, planting enormous quantities of flowers, hanging baskets and filling it with antiques.

Its massive four story white frame structure is skirted outside by a veranda filled with wicker furniture, a perfect spot for afternoon tea or a drink while watching the passing summer parade. Sooner or later everybody stops or passes by here.

The inn has been a favored watering hole of five presidents — Cleveland, McKinley, Theodore Roosevelt, Coolidge and Franklin D. Roosevelt. Nathaniel Hawthorne, William Cullen Bryant and Henry Wadsworth Longfellow were among the late great notables to stay here.

Inside are spacious public rooms filled with fine antiques, china collections, fresh flowers. The dining room, in plain view, serves quite good meals. See restaurant for details.

The 100 rooms upstairs which can accommodate 175 guests are all furnished differently, and vary in size. They all share one thing in common, however—their curtains, which are from "Country Curtains," an on-premise business which Mrs. Fitzpatrick runs.

All rooms are air conditioned, some have color TV, and of course, Norman Rockwell prints abound. Bedroom fireplaces, alas, are not used because of the age of the building.

Like all the very popular Berkshire places you will need reservations well in advance, but because this inn can accommodate so many, last minute cancellations often make it possible for the passerby to stay.

Pets are permitted, $7.50 extra.

The Widow Bingham Tavern inside the inn, and back patios are favorite gathering places in summer before Tanglewood concerts, the Lion's Den for after hours. The inn has an on-premise gift shop called the Pink Kitty.

Village Inn

Address:	Church Street, Lenox, Mass. 01240, 413-637-0020
Innkeepers:	Richard and Marie Judd
Rooms:	26 rooms, 15 baths
Rates:	July and August, $29-$47; Sept. and Oct. $25-$35; off season, $17-$29, double occupancy, meals not included.

Facilities: Located in the center of Lenox, one mile from Tanglewood. Dining room for breakfast and lunch. Pub downstairs for pre or after Tanglewood or apres ski warm up by the fire.

The Village Inn dates back to the 1700s and the American Revolution. It's been an operating inn for about 150 years.

The rooms are charming, each papered in different period wallpapers. The bedroom fireplaces, unfortunately, are off limits, but there's a warm fire downstairs in the lounge near to the bar, and in Poor Richard's pub, which is reminiscent of Benjamin Franklin's day with its hand hewn bar and church pew seats. Cocktails are served here afternoon and evening along with draught beer and wines, and light snacks.

A nice place for breakfast, New England flapjacks and syrup, with bacon or sausage, $2.85, Irish coffee to get you going, $1.65. Luncheon quiches, crepes, salads, burgers, overstuffed sandwiches, average $3.50.

Your hosts are congenial exurbanites who love innkeeping and as they put it, "if you can't be a house guest in the Berkshires, be ours."

Westbridge Inn

Address: Main Street, West Stockbridge, Mass., 01266, 413-232-7770

Innkeeper: Henricus G. A. Bergmans

Rooms: 14

Rates: $20 per night for double occupancy

Facilities: Dining room, tavern room and bar

This comfortable old restaurant and inn in the center of West Stockbridge village has a kind of Sunday-family-dinner feeling about it, quiet and unpretentious, but still "dress up" enough to feel special. That's just the way proprietor Henricus G.A. Bergmans, former innkeeper at the Red Lion Inn in Stockbridge, intends it to be... "a place for people to talk to each other."

Bergmans took over the Westbridge early in 1978 and reopened it after it had been closed for nearly a year. It had been mainly a night spot under previous owners. One of the first things he did was remodel the dining room, bringing it out of its second-fiddle status as a banquet area and dressing it up for company. The walls are all soft Williamsburg blue and the table settings glitter under candlelight.

The Westbridge menu offers a surprisingly large selection of fish and shellfish. Swordfish, scrod and bluefish, all with hollandaise; scallops in wine and garlic, mussels steamed in chablis and trout amandine were among the choices when we were there. There are also steaks, chops and the old reliable, Yankee pot roast.

Dinner is a la carte, with most entrees between $7.25 and $8.95.

You may also eat in the more informal tavern room, paneled in barnboard, with wooden booths and tables. Make your selections from a handwritten menu brought to your table on an easel.

The 14 guest rooms upstairs are simply furnished in colonial style with bright wallpapers, white bedspreads and braided rugs. Some have private baths. They're not fancy, but clean and comfortable, and at $20 a night for two, a best bargain.

Williamsville Inn

Address: Route 41, West Stockbridge, Mass., 01266, 413-274-6580

Innkeepers: Stuart and Lenora Bowen

Rooms: 12, all with private bath, some in nearby renovated barn and guest cottages. Dining rooms, all meals available.

Rates: $38-$48 summer; $28-$36 off season, double occupancy. Meals not included. On holidays a minimum stay of three days is required. Some rooms are reserved for stays of a week or longer. The inn closes for three weeks in November, one month in the spring.

Facilities: 10 landscaped acres, clay tennis court, heated swimming pool, pond for ice skating in winter, cross country skiing here and nearby marked trails.

Located on a quiet country road at the base of Tom Ball mountain, the inn was built in 1797 as a farmhouse and is the second oldest structure in what was called the hamlet of Williamsville. The area was settled by Elijah Williams, a descendant of Roger Williams of Rhode Island, and a half-brother to Emphraim Jr., who founded Williams College in Williamstown.

Now considered West Stockbridge, Williamsville today is no more than a group of seventeen white clapboard houses and one brick. There are no stores, no post office, the one room schoolhouse is now a private house.

The inn is seven miles from the center of Stockbridge, five minutes from Great Barrington and West Stockbridge shopping,

Willamsville Inn, West Stockbridge, Credit: Stephanie L. Johnson

fifteen minutes from the Berkshire Theatre and Tanglewood. Six miles away is downhill skiing at Butternut Basin.

Remodeled by its owners two years ago and redecorated in an 18th century style and mood with many family collected antiques, the inn has a charming country home-like feeling and seven working fireplaces.

The Bowens consider their inn, "a natural extension of our hobbies." "Lenny" is in charge of the kitchen. A gourmet cook, she favors country French provincial style cooking because, "it allows for more creativity."

Dining is in the "Main Dining Room," the adjacent "Library" or cheerful blue and white "Breakfast Room." Cosy fireplaces and flowering window boxes are rampant.

The inn's rooms are small, but bright, filled with hooked rugs, homemade afghans and collected family furnishings, and individual wallpapers.

The country restaurant is open to the public, we judged it among the top six best dining treats.

(See restaurants for details).

Note: Leave your pets at home.

MANSIONS

The Center at Foxhollow

Address:	Lenox, Mass., 01240, 413-637-2000; or toll free for reservations, 800-629-5990.
Rooms:	41, 20 with private baths, two suites with fireplaces, private baths and phones in main mansion. Additional cosy, but less posh, accommodations in two former guest houses and in renovated gate house.
Rates:	Per person includes full hearty breakfast and dinner, weekly lows of $30 with shared hall bath in guest houses, to weekend $46 and up at manor house. During summer weekends, a minimum of two nights stay required.
Facilities:	Sailing on Laurel Lake on the property, heated pool, tennis court, X country ski shop, trails on property, ice skating on frozen ponds and lake.

Formerly the home of Westinghouse and Vanderbilt families, then young ladies who once attended the now defunct Foxhollow School, the 285 acre estate is now a new spiffy resort frequented and favored by young urbanite couples who like their creature comforts.

Recently renovated, each room in the old Vanderbilt mansion is tastefully decorated. The book-lined library is a nicely fresh-minted deep green, the dining room a candlelight flattering apricot with navy blue cloths. A Hunt cocktail lounge which opens onto a patio carries out an English country feeling.

Owner-manager Donald Altshuler has blue print plans as well for additional condominums. He has aimed for a tone that is casual, but not informal. That means jackets in the dining room, but ties not de rigeur.

The food here is quite good. Vegetarians who like their gourmet fare predominately green are not forgotten.

The chef, formerly of the Red Lion Inn, brought his reputation and way with veal Oscar along with him.

Entrees for dinner average $9.50 beginning at $6.25 for the vegetarian platter to $11.50 for lamb chops or filet mignon with bernaise sauce. Fresh fish, baked stuffed shrimp with crabmeat stuffing, trout almondine are seaside worthy.

If you are not a houseguest, a call for dinner reservations is required.

Tanglewood picnickers can request a gourmet dinner complete

The Center at Foxhollow, Lenox, Credit: Stephanie L. Johnson

with blanket and wine.

Late night suppers Friday and Saturday by reservation. Entertainment late evenings in the library cum cabaret after dark.

Rolling lawns, landscaped gardens, sweeping vistas down to Laurel Lake, herbal walks and pine forests await your meandering or reflection.

Or you can saunter over to The Mount, Edith Wharton's former home, now occupied by Shakespeare and Co. which performs nightly in summer on the grounds.

Golf is available at nearby Cranwell. Arts and crafts classes and space to work in are offered in the property's barns.

Introductory mid-week package plans are available for six days, five nights, including nine gourmet meals, and lessons in golf, tennis, sailing. Price: from $140 to $180 per person double occupancy.

Gateways Inn and Restaurant

Address:	71 Walker Street, Lenox, Mass., 01240, 413-637-2532
Innkeepers:	Lilliane and Gerhard Schmid
Rooms:	10 double rooms, all with private bath, showers by 1979
Rates:	Winter midweek double room occupancy $28-$32, weekend, $32-$36. Summer midweek, $40-$65; Thursday-Sunday, $65-$80. Suite for one to four occupancy, $90 midweek; $140 weekends.
Facilities:	Center of town, minutes to Tanglewood.

This center of town mansion was the summer home of magnate Harley Proctor of Proctor and Gamble. Its Federal design brings to mind a bar of Ivory Soap, rectangular, clean, white and flat on top.

Owned now by Lilliane and Gerhard Schmid, each room, since they opened two years ago, has been renovated and repapered and carpeted. All the rooms are different, but all are extremely spacious with lovely huge old fashioned bathroom fixtures. Mrs. Schmid is presently adapting them for showers in case you'd rather not luxuriate in the huge, sometimes six foot long tubs.

The corner room, if you can grab it, or even catch a glimpse, rivals Blair House in Washington for splendid Victorian furnishings. Others are more modest in appointments, but elegant with their four poster mahogany beds.

The food here is excellent, (see restaurant listing). The chef, an award winning master of continental cuisine, once prepared a meal fit for a queen, and Queen Elizabeth got it.

The Schmids say summer weekends are sold out almost a year in advance, likewise some fall foliage weekends, but mid-week reservations are still possible almost any time of the year.

Both inn and restaurant are closed first two weeks in September.

Wheatleigh

Address:	P.O. Box 824, Lenox, Mass., 01240, 413-637-0610
Innkeepers:	A. David Weisgal; Florence Brooks-Dunay
Rooms:	18 bedrooms summer, 13 used in winter, wood burning fireplaces. Suites with terraces. Deluxe rooms reserved by week only. Breakfast included.

Rates:	$70-$100 summer weekends per couple; $45-$55 mid-week. Two night minimum winter; summer three night minimum.
Facilities:	Swimming pool and tennis court on the 22 acre estate. Patios, porticos, terraces, gardens, idyllic setting. Five minute jog to Tanglewood gate.

Some call it the most romantic inn in the Berkshires.

We would quibble only in that it's a palazzo really, not one's usual connotation of a Berkshire inn.

A villa that seems straight out of the Umbrian hills, it was built here by New York banker Henry Cook in 1893 as a wedding present to celebrate the marriage of his daughter to Carlos de Heredia, a Cuban count.

If you yearn to feel like a countess, this is the place to awaken in. It has an old world elegance recently freshened up with new paint and contemporary variations on Edwardian ambience. A circular enclosed gravel drive barely hints at what's inside. The entrance-living room centers about a massive carved fireplace where plushy couches bring you down to earth beneath high vaulted ceilings. A sweeping staircase pivots past exquisite pale pastel Tiffany-like windows, bowed gracefully now with age.

Patios, porticos, and terraces jut out over sweeping views of Stockbridge Bowl and the Berkshire hills.

Bedrooms are romantic visions of white dotted Swiss with canopies over the beds, interesting antiques. Lots of light and space and enough room to throw a small tea dance in the suites. In winter all beds have electric heated mattress pads. No need for air conditioning in summer.

Wheatleigh has a cosy small bar in the former library, gameroom downstairs and live entertainment weekends in Le Cave.

The dining room with its Victorian inspired claret walls, paintings, fireplace, and bentwood chairs, seems decoratively off key with the palazzo's Italian and Belle Epoque feeling, but it adds an informality that isn't a glaring discord.

The menu here is eclectic. It is a potpourri that changes nightly. You may find stir fried vegetables and organic brown rice with Japanese tofu for the vegetarian inclined, shrimp in lobster sauce, veal birds, sole Florentine, scampi, coq au vin, or whatever else the cook choses as an on-going adventure. Always fresh vegetables. Entrees range $8-$12.50 and are served to outside guests by reservation. Desserts include fresh fruits, homemade cakes, Camambert cheese, creme brulee and the host's own cheesecake.

A counter, but cultured, balance to the imposing character of Wheatleigh are its urbane host and hostess who are just as at home padding about in jeans or parkas as they are operating as lord and lady of the manor.

Wheatleigh opened for weekend villa viewers three summers ago, and if it is the palazzo you wish to park in you are advised to book well in advance. Reservations are on the books a year ahead. Most guests snag their next season at check out time.

Eastover

Address:	East Street, off Rtes. 7 and 20, Lenox, Mass. 01240, 413-637-0625
Innkeeper:	George G. Bisacca
Rooms:	170 rooms, accommodations for 500, various style "cottages" in buildings on grounds
Rates:	Weekends, $31-$44 per person; weekdays, $32 per person, includes three meals
Facilities:	Indoor and outdoor swimming pools, sauna, own stables, seven tennis courts, novice to intermediate ski slopes with chair and rope tows, golf driving ranges, rifle, archery.

Eastover Resort, Lenox, Credit: Stephanie L. Johnson

From the outside iron fence and brick gate one imagines the restraint of a Georgian country estate.

The big house, formerly owned by a New York stock broker, is in fact, Georgian and imposing, but it is surrounded by the most diverse mixture of housing accommodations we've ever seen.

There are replica ranch houses, southern plantation colonials and modern cabins.

The surrounding property and activities at this 1600 acre

resort are just as varied. You'll find Indian teepees, old fire engines, fenced in deer, longhorn steers, buffalo, donkeys, swans and ducks, to delight children, lots of outdoor lawn games, shuffleboard set up for adults.

This is a very informal place and Mr. Bisacca planned it that way. If you can't tell from the names he's chosen for the variety of buildings, names like Carolinian, Jackson, Virginian, Jeb Stuart, Grant, he is enamoured with the Civil War. You'll find his own personal American Heritage Museum here also.

Special weekends and weeks have been organized for singles, couples, families. Children under 18 are not allowed on weekends except for the special family weekends which are very popular.

There are buffets, cookouts, happy hours, costume parties, barn dances, hay rides, seasonal beerfests, reunion weeks and weekends.

Reservations are often booked a year in advance for chosen weekends.

Pets can be accommodated on the property at no extra charge, but you care for them yourself in separate bowser-like kennels.

Jug End

Address:	South Egremont, Mass., 01258, 413-528-0434
Rooms:	130 most with bath, some shared, various style accommodations in several buildings on property as well as in the big barn main building
Rates:	$44-$52 in season; $35-$42 off season per person double occupancy includes breakfast and dinner
Facilities:	Tennis, (3 indoor, 2 out) 18 hole par 70 golf course, indoor and outdoor swimming pools, saunas, own stables and woodland trails, all winter sports, Alpine skiing for novices, Nordic skiing on trails for all levels, ice skating on pond, trout fishing, skeet shooting, hiking. Five minutes to Catamount ski slopes, one half hour to Tanglewood.

Of all the Berkshire four season, all encompassing, self contained resorts, Jug End with its 1200 acres nestling in Guilder Hollow at the foot of Mt. Everett offers the most natural beauty.

The property is exquisite in fall when the hills are ablaze with color.

Accommodations vary from the rural warmth of the big barn, to balconied rooms in 18th century cottages, or economy priced colorful basic rooms, also apartments and suites with kitchenettes.

The main building, or big barn, has a hunting lodge feeling with its toasty fireplace, red plaid carpeting and bowls of polished apples scattered about for armchair munching.

Jug End aims to attract people who want sophisticated informality and leans to couples and families.

Country style cooking, smorgasbords, clam bakes, steaks and prime ribs are the basic fare here.

Whether you are an active sports enthusiast or a contemplative nature lover, Jug End has equal appeal.

Oak n' Spruce

Address:	Off Route 2, South Lee, Mass., 01260, 413-243-3500, toll free: 800-628-5072
Rooms:	65 motel rooms with view, double beds, bath
Rates:	$28-$35 per person double occupancy, midweek; $60-$70 weekends, includes breakfast and dinner.
Facilities:	Indoor and outdoor swimming pools, two clay tennis courts, 9 hole golf, Frisbee golf, novice ski slopes, ski instructors, rentals, cross country skiing, tobaganning, ice skating, snowmobiling.

Situated on 440 acres adjoining 12,000 belonging to Beartown State Forest, this resort is like its own self contained little village offering a smorgasbord of activities that promises something for everybody.

Ten buildings house the air conditioned guest rooms. Community lounges, game rooms, saunas and whirpool bath are in the main building.

Outdoor meals, barbeques and buffet extravaganzas and planned socials aim for an informal style that appeals to singles and couples who want to mingle socially with others.

The views here are lovely. Rooms do not have either television or phones, the better to escape.

You can get here directly by metropolitan buses and don't need a car once you are here. But if you plan to take in the nearby south county sights you will need one.

Package plans are available, as are family and group rates.

The Berkshire Hilton Inn

Address: Berkshire Common, Pittsfield, Mass., 01201, 413-499-2000

Rooms: 175 guest rooms and suites

Rates: Single $28-$38 off season, double $36-$44. Summers, anticipate $48-$58

Facilities: Swimming pool, saunas, two restaurants, bar-lounge, top of the common views. Center of town location, equi-distant to north as well as south county attractions.

One of three Berkshire county hotels, the Berkshire Hilton Inn is neither a motel, nor inn, in the true sense of either. Too big to be a motel, too individual to be compared to a Holiday Inn, too contemporary to be an inn, the Hilton has to be considered in a class by itself at the top of the small list that includes the Treadway Williams Inn in Williamstown, and the Sheraton Inn in North Adams.

Opened in 1970 the Hilton got off to a slow start, but a switch in ownership brought about an infusion of enthusiasm and some smart snappy redecorating. Now stylish without being troublesomely trendy, the Hilton has a lot of appeal for weekend urbanites, and traveling businessmen.

The poolside dining terrace is an inviting place to come for lunch munchers who favor crisp sandwiches $2.75 for most, and green garden salads tossed out in combinations from $2.25-$3.95. Open year round 7 a.m.-3 p.m., breakfast too; summer 11-1 a.m. light snacks after concerts.

There's also the Branding Iron a pub-like steak, chicken sirloin saloon, entrees from $4.50-$9.95 include as many runs as you want around the salad bar.

In summer Jonathan's, an otherwise banquet-business room becomes a seafood restaurant with entrees from $6.75 for seafood newburgh to $8.50 for broiled swordfish.

Upstairs the Emerald Room done in shades of green, upholstered printed chairs and emerald walls, sparkles as a year round night spot with a weekend band and vocalist, wrap around windows overlooking Pittsfield. It's the closest thing to a big city feeling found in the Berkshires.

The bedrooms at the Hilton are superior to nondescript motel modern with their contemporary fabrics and warm color tones. TV, of course and the usual hotel-motel amenities with the addition of a businessman's bonus that serves up the morning paper with coffee in your room after wake up.

The Hilton has skiiers packages in winter, is near to Bousquet, Butternut, about 45 minutes to Brodie and Jiminy, an hour to Catamount.

In summer, figure 40 minutes to either summer theatre or Tanglewood.

Sheraton-North Adams Inn

Address: 40 Main St., North Adams, Mass., 01247, 413-664-4561

Innkeeper: Edward Bandar, owner-manager

Rooms: 102 rooms, air conditioned, six suites, meeting and banquet rooms

Rates: $29.50-$49.50 double occupancy, not including meals

Facilities: Heated indoor swimming pool, bar, lounge, dining room, terrace used in summer, entertainment and dancing Thursday-Saturday. Breakfast, lunch, dinner and brunch

Located in the downtown of North Adams, three miles from Harriman Airport, 15 minute drive to Williamstown Theatre Festival and Clark Art Institute, one hour to Tanglewood.

The rooms are spacious, air conditioned, contemporary furnishings.

The menu is basic sirloin, scrod, scallops, pork chops and prime ribs which are available in three sizes; eight ounce, three quarters of a pound, or a full pound. Prices are $5.25-$11.25. All entrees are served with potato, vegetable, rolls and butter. Salad bar. Soups change daily.

The Treadway Williams Inn

Address: Corner of Routes 7 and 2, Williamstown, Mass., 01267, 413-458-9371 or toll free: 800-631-0812

Rooms: 104 rooms, 5 suites, banquet and meeting rooms

Rates: $32-$42 double occupancy, meals not included

Facilities: Heated indoor swimming pool, saunas, dining room for breakfast, lunch and dinner, bar, lounge. Entertainment weekends, disco weekends, dining al fresco on the terrace in summer.

The Treadway Williams Inn falls into the category we are calling motor hotels.

Located within a half a block of the Williamstown Theater Festival, the Clark Art Institute, the center of town, within 15 minutes drive to two major ski areas (Brodie and Jiminy Peak) this inn has an ideal location.

It's new, the rooms are comfortable, air conditioned and modern.

A warm and cheerful lobby with fireplace and English antiques greets you upon entering. The scarlet dining room peeks around the corner from the lounge.

Homestyle soups, crocks of chowder, French onion au gratin, salads, club and deli sandwiches, burgers and quiche are offered on the luncheon menu, as well as heftier house specials like turkey pot pie with salad bowl, $2.75.

Evening entrees range from $5.65 to $9.25 for mainstay dishes like chicken, veal Parmigiano, fish, steak or turkey and include appetizer, potato or vegetable, salad bar, fresh baked bread, dessert and beverage.

3. DINING OUT

Candlelight Inn and Restaurant

Address: 53 Walker Street, Lenox, Mass., 01240, 413-637-1555

Innkeeper: James De Mayo, owner, manager, chef

Open: Lunch and dinner, 11:30-2:30; 5-10 p.m. Sunday dinner only. Closed Tuesday except during July and August

Facilities: Dining room, bar

A Colonial style restaurant that is tastefully decorated, warm and comfortable with subdued lighting, candlelight, of course, per its name. Al fresco garden dining in summer.

The menu is "Continental" and the country it leans toward most heavily is Italy, but this is far from just an Italian food choice. The entrees number two dozen, everything from sauteed frog legs meuniere to calves sweet breads au beurre noir and ragouts of veal. Veal and fish lovers will find the choices particularly tempting.

Entrees are priced from $6.95-$25, most between $7.50 and $9.

Chef De Mayo believes in "cooking from the old school," meaning vegetables are fresh, they bone their own veal and chicken, make homemade soups daily.

Desserts are nothing special here, so don't be expecting Italian pastries. It's the main entree you are after here, and it is very good.

For appetizers you might try oysters a la Rockefeller, $3.95, shrimp and oyster cocktail, zuppa de clams, cherrystones. Choice of homemade soup du jour, juice or chicken liver pate with dinner.

Entrees include poached fillet of fresh Brunswick Salmon hollandaise, $9.50; baked jumbo scampi in garlic butter, half a dozen different veal dishes.

Desserts include chocolate mousse, peach melba, parfaits, apple pie, Irish coffee, expresso, Darjelling tea.

Wine by the bottle, carafe or American wine by the glass leans to best known favorites.

Minimum at dinner of $6.95.

The mid-day lunch fare runs from poached eggs Benedict to

beefsteak and kidney pie, casserole of veal Marengo, scallops, haddock, chef's salad, crepes, priced at a $3.50 average. Also hefty sandwich plates beginning at $2.25. There is a minimum charge at lunch of $2.

Gateways Inn and Restaurant

Address: 71 Walker Street, Lenox, Mass., 01240, 413-637-2532

Innkeepers: Lilliane and Gerhard Schmid

Open: Dinner, Tuesday-Sunday. Closed Monday, Also Tuesday in winter. Brunch Sunday 11 a.m.-2 p.m. Dinner 5:30-9 p.m. midweek, till 9:30 p.m. weekends. Both inn and restaurant are closed first two weeks of September.

Formerly the summer home of Harley Procter of Procter and Gamble, the Gateways, now owned and run by Lilliane and Gerhard Schmid, has earned a prestigious name for culinary excellence in just two seasons.

The cuisine is continental, but some of the best dishes are German rather than French.

Chef Schmid is the winner of a gold and silver medal in the 1967 International Culinary Competition in Frankfort, West Germany, and received three culinary Olympic gold medals in 1976. His meals are fit for a queen. He did, in fact, prepare lunch for Queen Elizabeth II when she visited Boston for the Bicentennial.

The food here is excellent. The atmosphere is old world elegant. You dine in two adjoining terra cotta rooms with fireplaces and floor to ceiling windows. The Venetian mantle high floor lamps in one room are lovely. If you listen you can hear the chimes from the Episcopal Church on the corner, every hour.

Prices for entrees range from $6.95-$12.95 semi a la carte which includes fresh vegetables and salad. The only foods frozen here are shrimps and ice cream. Soups, like the cream of spinach, are superb.

The filet of sole saute Washington with fresh chunks of lobster, lobster sauce garnished with hollandaise is delicious. Our second choice might have been veal Wisconsin, a rich sauteed and ground veal stuffed with cheese, added to a veal scallop all baked in butter covered with Maderia. Or maybe it would have been shrimp Andreas stuffed with crabmeat, veal and mushrooms.

Save room for their sumptuous desserts. House specialties include Viennese apple strudle, Kaluah cheese cake, grasshopper pie and a three layer cake called Black Forest Cake. A large choice of over a dozen coffees, expresso, cappucino to savor and sip. The foreign wine list here is good.

Sunday's brunch could set you up for the day. There's Wiener Schnitzel, French toast Monte Carlo, seafood crepes, a veal cutlet rolled in egg batter sauteed in sweet cream butter, home fries, salad, $6.75.

If you'd like to cook like they do take note: there is a cooking school here, cost $400 for a week includes room and board. Commuters' week-long classes are $125, Sept. Jan. and April, all food provided. Complete dinners are made each time, from soup to dessert.

The Schmids are undecided about recommending reservations for dinner. When it is crowded they can not hold tables. Best advice: call first, they may be accepting summer reservations at appointed seating times as a way around the dilemma.

Le Country Restaurant

Address: 52 North Street, Williamstown, Mass., 01267, 413-458-4000

Open: Lunch, 11:30-2 p.m.; dinner, 5-9 p.m. seven days a week except Friday and Saturday, dinner only

The Country Restaurant serves 120 in three small dining rooms, but the feeling you get here, particularly in the room with the fireplace, is of a small country restaurant.

The chef-owner Raymond Canales was born in Spain, and is an experienced chef in the continental tradition.

Homemade soups, always a cream and a clear, and fresh vegetables in season from Sam Smith's Caretaker Farm in Hancock, where they are organically grown, are served here.

The luncheon menu includes coquilles St. Jacques at $4.95, chicken livers saute with mushrooms, curried shrimp, fettucine a la Romana, as well as omelettes, several cold plates and sandwiches, steaks, turkey and chicken. Vegetable and salad included.

Evening menu offers a choice of 25 entrees, $7.95-$12.50. Veal and fish dishes are our favorites. They buy their own legs of veal to make scallopine al marsala with mushrooms and veal cutlet Cazadora baked with tomato sauce and cheese. Stuffed shrimp, shrimp curry, lemon sole meuniere and the ubiquitous scampi are delivered twice a week from the Boston markets, but the fish dishes that caught our attention are Spanish in derivation: Lenquado con Champana, fresh lemon sole rolled. and poached in champagne sauce, $10.95, and Cazuela de Mariscos, a seafood casserole of crab, lobster and sole served in wine sauce.

The dessert menu has a half dozen ice creams and parfaits, flan, baba au rhum, and Spanish cream, a light custard served with brandied peaches and whipped cream. Espresso is available.

Reservations recommended.

Le Jardin, Williamstown, Credit: Stephanie L. Johnson

Le Jardin

Address:　　　　Route 7, Williamstown, Mass., 01267, 413-458-8032

Open:　　　　Lunch, dinner, Sunday brunch Closed Tuesday. Winter, no lunch; summer, open seven days from 11:30-9:30 p.m.

A gracious country inn set in a pine grove, Le Jardin is a little garden spot of French eating that nestles near a small pond.

We don't know where else you can find Malosol caviar, crisp Long Island duckling flambee in cognac, or steak tartare.

Chef and owner Walter Hayn told us he has a special use for the day's left over hollandaise. He makes cookies out of it, which tells you something about how Mr. Hayn approaches his kitchen; nothing wasted, but everything fresh daily.

There is a bar here and nine rooms and eight baths upstairs, neither highly publicized. It's the food Mr. Hayn concentrates on.

Classic French cooking, with a choice of a dozen entrees that average $12.50 each served with soup of the day, potato, fresh garden vegetables and salad with house dressing.

There's chicken with mushrooms in a light wine cream sauce and pastry shell for $8.50, tender sweetbreads in a light curry sauce in pastry shell, $12, veal chop in mornay sauce on a bed of leaf spinach, $12, plus steaks with bernaise sauce, prime ribs, or tournedos bordelaise served on butter croutons for $12.

Delicious lemon mousse, fresh fruits, baked Alaska and cherries jubilee among the desserts.

Sunday brunch is a generous buffet of multiple choice for $5.75 and you can go back again and again for more.

This is actually an inn, although very few people know it. Mr. Hayn is in the process of redoing the upstairs rooms, papering and stripping one at a time. Parents of college students know about them and rent them well in advance as they are, which Mr. Hayn admits is nothing special yet. One family we know, who have a long line of Williams alumni, return year after year and rent out the entire floor. The price is $16 for a single, $24 for a double.

The Mill on the Floss

Address: Route 7, New Ashford, Mass., 01237, 413-458-9123

Open: Dinners, seven days a week 5-10 p.m.

It looks like an unpretentious house set off from the road, but the cooking that sallies forth from its open-face kitchen is widely acknowledged to be among the best, if not the top of the mark in Berkshire County.

Go in one winter evening early in the week and see if you can count the number of restaurant owners who stop by here to eat. And no wonder! Chef owner Maurice Champagne makes dishes befitting his name — they sparkle.

He makes especially delicious veal dishes, and also quenelle of sole, frogs legs Provencal, sweetbreads au beurre noire, beef Wellington, to name a few. Entrees here are $7.50 up to $22, with most in the $8.50 range.

"When you cook seven days a week sometimes you have bad days. Please do me a favor and soft pedal the praise," he cautioned. We listened, We heard. But we doubt it. He can flip out a quenelle of sole in white wine sauce the way the rest of us poor souls can, with luck, poach a perfect egg.

"Well," says Mr. Champagne, "I've been cooking since I was 12."

His dining room is very French country kitchen with beamed ceiling, open kitchen in plain view where you can see him busily at work, the warm glow of a bright plethora of hanging copper pots, a fire in the fireplace, crockery and candlelight. It reminds us of a restaurant we know on L'ile d'Orleans, in Quebec, an unspoiled little island which hasn't changed much since the French first settled in to farm it in the 1700s. Not surprisingly we found he is French Canadian and came to the Berkshires 25 years ago from Montreal.

A thoroughly modern man, his cooking gets down to the bare bones from which he makes all his sauces. He's choosey when he selects. Vegetables too are carefully selected, organically grown and bought from Samuel Smith who owns Caretaker Farm in Hancock. He is as painstaking over his produce as Mr. Champagne is with his dishes.

The night we last popped by two customers blew in out of the winter wind twenty minutes after closing time.

"We don't want dinner," they explained, noticing the clock on the wall. "Couldn't we just have a few quenelles? Just maybe a salad, some soup," they begged.

Mr. Champagne, obviously weary at 10:30 p.m., smiled and obliged.

Two minutes later they bounded back. Please would he also write down the recipe?

"I really don't think you would be satisfied," he told them patiently. "I don't cook from a recipe. It's always just a little bit different," he smiled.

It's hard to find a pinch of inspiration at the supermarket spice counter. It's even harder to distill his to go.

New Boston Inn

Address:	Junction of Routes 8 and 57, Sandisfield, Mass., 01255, 413-258-4511
Open:	Dinner and Sunday brunch year-round. Closed Monday and Tuesday. Sunday hours from 1-5 p.m.

Wonderful smells from the kitchen waft through the house as you enter this one-time inn, now a restaurant and private home that dates back to 1750.

Three generations live here and all have a hand in the kitchen from mother to daughter to granddaughter.

And what a hand. The food here was a delightful surprise. Dishes we've never encountered anywhere else in the Berkshires. These ladies really love to cook and try new things

Dining here is like dining in someone's private country home dining room — cosy, comfortable and well attended to.

Reservations are a must because it is small and word of mouth surely travels.

We did, from the northwestern most tip of Massachusetts to this corner in the eastern most part of Berkshire county, a hop-skip from the Connecticut border. It took about an hour plus to get here, but worth it. South county residents and second home owners from New York and nearby Connecticut frequent this restaurant. From New York the weekend commute is only two hours, a fact that's caused the Sandisfield Planning Commission to regard their little town as "one of the last lungs left around New York."

So far it is unchoked, a charming little town which is the largest in the county in land mass, 52.5 square miles, and one of the smallest in population, 600.

All that remains of the old Sandisfield are a few old white houses and the suggestion of a village green. Now second homes are tucked away off the 84 miles of town roads and there are cleared fields, thicket lilacs, one post office and two general stores and this special little place.

Sandisfield has an interesting history, but that's another story, or better yet, ask the ladies.

We started our meal here with homemade vegetable soup followed by chopped veal en Croute $8.75, ground veal stuffed with mozarella cheese in a puff pastry smothered in mushroom wine sauce. Excellent. For dessert, grandma's Berkshire pudding, a sumptuous rich chocolate mousse with chopped nuts added. It's grandma's recipe and she just wanted to name it after the Berkshires. Fresh vegetables, potato, salad, dinner, with a glass of wine, dessert and coffee, $12.56.

Appetizers are tempting and this night included pate maison cornichons, a goose liver spread served with tiny pickles, $3.50, shrimp remoulade, artichoke hearts a la Greque.

Entrees average $8.75. Other choices, which vary nightly, always offer two kinds of steaks, crepes, fish, chicken. Perhaps fresh sole Nantua, a cream sauce with shrimp, curry shrimp madras, boneless breast of chicken picatta, chicken livers sauteed with herbs and Maderia.

The Sandisfield Historical Society has put out a charming little book titled "Sandisfield Cookery," containing local recipes, some from grandma, along with interesting local history. Ask to see a copy, if it's not out on a foyer table.

If you should want a drink before dinner and there's a bit of a wait, the sitting room off the dining room, an elegant family living room with fireplace, is a public room.

The Old Mill

Address:　　　　Route 23, South Egremont, Mass. 01258, 413-528-1421

Open:　　　　Lunch and dinner. Lunch, Friday, Saturday, Sunday. Dinner from 5:30 p.m. Closed Tuesday. Bar parlor open for drinks and sandwiches

A newcomer to the Berkshires, summer of '78 being its first, the Old Mill is situated in exactly what it sounds like... an old grist mill and adjacent blacksmith shop built in 1797.

While the water wheel which churned up water from Hubbard Brook out back has long since gone, if you look closely you can still see remnants of its more humble origins.

Terry and Juliet Moore, who live upstairs, spent two years gutting the building, installing a perfectly charming restaurant and bar parlor.

The blacksmith once shod his horses in what is now the dining room. The forge, still intact, is a fireplace used in winter. The wide floorboards have been carefully restored where possible, hand stenciled where they were too far gone. If you look closely you can see hoofprints and the marks made by the smithy's sparks which once scattered across the wide floorboards. In the beams are all sorts of cut-outs where hay was stored.

The feeling now is of an old English pub atmosphere tastefully interpreted in a Shaker idiom of simplicity and embellished with Terry's authentic autographed picture collection of Longfellow, Wellington, Lloyd George and Kipling. Juliet's collections of old mincers, cabbage cutters, green china and English Majolica leaf plates adorn the white plaster walls and cupboards.

Terry, who is English, has always been in the restaurant business and began at the age of 16 on board Cunard ships. He also put his feet down for a time in San Francisco, Pennsylvania and New York City restaurants.

The menu here has been chosen with the same deliberate care put into the restoration. It varies, fish dishes depend upon availability of fresh fish, for instance. Usually you will find a chicken dish, calves liver, prime ribs, lamb chops, veal piccata, scampi. We had a delicious chicken in tarragon cream sauce for $6.95. Prices range from $4.95-$10.75 and include house salad, fresh vegetable and potato.

Everything is fresh. Hot fresh breads and homemade soups such as minestrone are tasty. A small, but select, wine list ranges in price from $4.75 to $9.75.

Save room for the desserts which are yummy. Goodies like Stilton apple and port, profiterole au chocolate, meringue surprise which is a confection of fresh strawberries or fruit, vanilla ice cream, whipped cream and shredded fresh chocolate.

In summer you may lunch on the sundeck overlooking the brook. Luncheon prices start at $2.95 to $5.25 for omelettes, sandwiches, hamburger and salad nicoise, broiled filet of sole, crepes.

Reservations are accepted for groups of five or more only.

A close hop for the Salisbury, Connecticut, crowd, the Old mill is now enjoying a following from both states. From north county it takes about an hour to get here. Worth the trip.

Red Lion Inn

Address: Route 102, Stockbridge, Mass., 01262, 413-298-5545

Open:: Breakfast, lunch and dinner. Dining al fresco in the garden courtyard, elegantly in the dining room, or a cosy corner in the dimly lit Widow Bingham Tavern. Late drinks and sandwiches, entertainment weekends at the Lion's Den. Tea, cocktails or cordials on the veranda

This landmark center of town inn also has a reputation for good country and continental cooking.

Entrees range from $3 to $3.50 for luncheon sandwich or salads, dinners from $10 to $17 for a choice from 21 entrees.

Different daily soups like a cream of watercress, puree of turnip and apple, sweet vegetable with cheese, breads and homebaked pies.

Several fish choices, two veal dishes, the veal Oscar our favorite, steaks, lamb or pork chops, prime ribs and an entrecote with herb butter, or if you're feeling flush, chateaubriand for two served with sauce Choron and garnish of fresh vegetables, $30. Always a salad included.

Desserts are classic country favorites like apple pie with cheddar cheese, pecan pie, New England pudding, cheesecake with apricot glaze.

Fresh flowers at each table and a scorn for the frozen and plastic, plus the fact that this is THE place to see and be seen account in part for some of the popularity.

Reservations are advised for the dining room. You can walk out back for a garden drink or light snack before Tanglewood and wait for a table. If it's super crowded, which isn't unusual, pass time meandering among the chic little shops in the mews nearby.

The garden plantings, baskets of fuscia and banks of colorful impatiens are a burst of joyful color in summer.

The front veranda with its wicker chairs, couches and flowered cushions is our idea of a perfect spot for tea.

The Springs

Address: Route 7, New Ashford, Mass., 01237, 413-458-3465

Open: Lunch and dinner daily, 11:30-10:30 p.m.

For 48 years three generations of the Grosso family have been introducing dishes to Berkshirites. It was they who first served the baked stuffed clam, escargots bourguignonne, and zuppa de clams to the area.

The Springs today, rebuilt after a fire gutted the interior three years ago, is more attractive than ever.

The Grosso's, who are Italian from the Piedmont part of northern Italy, have chosen Italian as well as classic French cuisine on which to build their reputation.

There are 28 entrees listed on the regular menu and an additional daily choice for "our true gourmets" that introduces one dish each day. Entrees average $8.50.

The most common complaint you'll hear about The Springs is: "But they serve so much food." Actually, it's just very difficult to practice restraint beginning with their antipastos and relishes followed by their amply portioned entrees. Most people read the menu with their eyes and forget their stomaches.

Seafood is fresh twice a week, veal dishes are especially good, vegetables are fresh in season, some frozen in winter, breads are baked on the premises in winter, bought from a baker in summer when the kitchen is way too busy. Pastries like puff shells, crepes, biscuit short cakes, yum, come straight out of the kitchen.

For appetizers we love the hearts of artichoke with proscuitto, vinaigrette, $2.95 or baked stuffed clams done The Springs' own way. But maybe a fresh fruit cup with sherbet, 75 cents, is wisest if you think ahead.

Want to close your eyes and eat in Rome? Order the Fettuccine Carbonara, pasta with a creamy white sauce and fresh Parmesan cheese. Like veal, but want something more flamboyant than a delicate picatta? Try veal Oscar, sauteed fillets and Belgian asparagus topped with lobster, $9.95. There's also chicken Cacciatore simmered in their special wine sauce, filet of sole Veronique baked with grapes in a wine cream sauce, $9.50, and if you want to sink your teeth into steak try steak Dianne flamed in cognac sauce.

Undecided, take a stab; you aren't likely to be stung by disappointment.

If you've managed to save room for dessert there are cherries jubilee, chocolate mousse with creme de Cacao and Luxuro, a sinful chocolate cake topped with ice cream, cream and chocolate sauce. No room, try espresso followed by a coffee liqueur served in a tiny edible chocolate glass.

If you're wondering how they do it, just ask, recipes are shared. And at the gift shop across the street, next to the motel the family also runs, you can buy their own chutney, antipasto and goodies.

Imported French wines by the glass or bottle are offered.

The wood paneled, high vaulted dining room with its huge chandeliers, booths and well spaced tables and the red lounge near the bar with its glowing fireplace, offer a warm welcome in winter.

There is a sense of calm and unhurried dining made possible by a superbly organized and outfitted kitchen where a half dozen chefs meticulously work at their own islands, stoves, and counters. On a busy night Mr. Grosso says they can turn out 1,000 meals because everything they need is within the reach of a mere pivot.

Stockbridge Station Restaurant

Address: South off Main Street, Route 7, Stockbridge, Mass., 01262, 413-298-3402

Open: 7 days a week in summer, dinner sittings at 5:30 and 9 p.m.; lunch, 11-3; Sunday brunch, noon-4; tea, 3:30-5 p.m.; open winter weekends, a la carte

Open for its first season summer of 1978, this restaurant and cocktail lounge in a gutted and renovated Stanford White railroad station has swiftly earned an envied reputation as the choicest of watering holes.

Stockbridge Station, Stockbridge, Credit: Stephanie L. Johnson

There's a feeling of smart sophistication coupled with an atmosphere Humphrey Bogart and Ingrid Bergman would have loved, if only they could have gotten out of Casablanca.

Passenger trains have long since stopped passing by here, it's strictly freight that lumbers by twice a day on the tracks outside, but inside the going is strictly first class.

And with dinners priced at $15.95-$19.95 for a complete five-course dinner you would expect something more than tourist class. You get it here.

There is one entree per evening and it varies daily. Jamaican born chef and manager Norma Shirley and her partner, Celta Vassel, believe it is best to do one thing at a time superbly. They also want their customers to feel they are dining in someone's home. Add these aims together with what they serve up and you have an exceptional dining experience.

On a given evening you may find Canneloni, lamb, Jamaican or third world specialties, Mediterranean food, quail or whatever their fancy dictates. There is always fresh fish Thursday when it is delivered from Maine. Obviously, it is best to call ahead if you want to play it safe, also de rigeur if you want to secure a reservation.

We had a choice of hot cream of zucchini soup or a delicious cold tomato soup blended with oregano and brandy, served over ice in a glass bowl with a dollup of sour cream. Delicious. Two quails served in white wine and brandy sauce with white grapes, fresh string beans with slivered almonds and rice. A salad of eight cherry tomatoes (peeled) with vinaigrette, very delicate. A choice of brie, camembert or goat cheese followed. Next were slices of pears and canteloupe, fresh, of course. For dessert, a peach cobbler won out over an Amaretto torte or fruit in kirsch only because two stomachs aren't provided to diners. The station has a special pastry chef. And to savor, several cups of Jamaican Blue Mountain coffee.

The portions were adequate, not overwhelming or skimpy. Breads are homemade like zucchini bread served warm in small metal baskets with accompanying glass crock of butter. The effect is glistening. The wine list offers a small but good selection available also by half carafe. Teas, if you are a teetotaler, are blended especially by Simpson and Vail.

The dining room has 11 round butcher block tables elegantly set with beige linen cloths and ribbon tied napkins. Lighting is subdued and candles are at each table.

The walls of the station are exposed brick. Overhead a working fan purrs. An old wooden railroad luggage cart is filled with ferns and serves as a divider between entry and lounge at the right where a bar and piano player serve up their medleys. Lots of plants and strikingly tropical looking bouquets of vivid gladiolas give a hint of lush Jamaica. Summertime drinks such as sumptuous daiquiris and fruit concoctions add to the feeling.

Tea is served 3:30-5 p.m. English style with pastries and scones or finger sandwiches, $4.50-$5.50.

Sunday brunch for omelettes, quiches, pancakes, range from $1.50-$5.50.

A screened outdoor dining room on the station's platform is used in summer.

Mrs. Shirley moved up here from New York with her doctor husband. She has cooked for years and spotted the railroad station as a potential place to stop visitors in their tracks. The building itself is owned by actor Terrance Hill and his wife.

She knew the big city concept of one entree at a time was new to the Berkshires, but she took the chance. Last summer the station was crowded weekends through fall foliage for dinner. There were turn aways, proving, even with the price of the ticket, this station is worth the stop no matter where you're bound.

Williamsville Inn

Address: Route 41, West Stockbridge, Mass., 01266,
                 413-274-6580
Innkeepers: Stuart and Lenora, "Lenny", Bowen
Open: Dinner, candlelight dining 6-9 p.m. except
                 Sunday, 4 to 8 p.m.

This charming country inn specializes in country French provincial style cooking.

Entrees begin at $7.75 and range to $12, with most averaging $8.75. Appetizers include Mrs. Bowen's country pate maison, $1.75, also langoustines, salmon mousse, quiche or escargots. We had a sampling of all, our favorite being the salmon mousse.

Paupiette of chicken with artichokes, mushrooms and gruyere stuffing was our choice. A real delight. Other choices include crabmeat Bienville, coquille St. Jacques, steak au poivre, veal Francaise.

Desserts like mocha ice cream torte, apple pie Normandy, fudge nut torte, cheesecake Williamsville, make you wish you had two stomachs. Spanish, Irish and Dutch coffees and expresso are offered. The wine list is select and pleasing.

All breads (the lemon bread is yummy and made by the Bowens' daughter), popovers, and desserts are home made. Vegetables are fresh. Herbs are used subtly and skillfully. Breakfast guests at the inn will find fresh squeezed orange juice. Nothing is from a mix. The salad vinaigrette is tasting and appealing with its little slivers of sliced beets.

Mrs. Bowen, who is both innkeeper and chef, believes in graciously presented meals.

"People dine with their eyes before they eat," she says.

The dining room is small, serves 36, at clothed tables under a beamed ceiling. Windows look out over flower boxes in summer. The fireplace roars in winter. A small library-like adjoining room is also used for dinner and seats 24. The cheerful country fresh blue and white breakfast room, sometimes used for evening meals, seats 16. Outside dining in summer on a screened porch.

A small room with tables and bar as you enter has been dubbed the tavern. You can have a pre-dinner drink here or sit around the fireplace.

August Moon

Address: 54 State Road, Route 7, Great Barrington, Mass., 01230, 413-528-9363

Open: Lunch and dinner. Closed Tuesday. Brunch on Sunday. Dinners 5:30-10 p.m. Lunch 12-4 p.m.

Small, informal and modestly priced, The August Moon is a bright spot for adventuresome food lovers.

Eight tables seat 25 in this little house whose maroon lacquered walls and lamps hint of art deco.

This is a no-additive, natural food place, and a Chinese food spa.

Carol and Joe Carini are new in the restaurant business, two ex-urbanites who carried their love of cooking with them to the country a year ago. Joe used to manage his father's trattoria in Little Italy, New York. Carol studied Chinese cooking for a year for fun. Together they are managing to make this place grow as fast as a bean sprout.

The menu is varied and, except for basic sandwiches, changes constantly. Soups are always homemade. There's chili, quiche, abundant salads in summer with homemade mayonnaise, and thick, especially baked for them, breads.

Every night they offer close to eight or nine different Mandarin, Cantonese, and Szechuan dishes, and at least three vegetable entrees.

Their desserts are uniquely their own. There are gingerbread, carob brownies, carrot layer cake, Mom's cheesecake and lemon squares and a dozen different teas to choose from.

Entrees cost $4 to $6. Quiches average $1.60, soup cups 95 cents, sandwiches $1.50. Desserts are 95 cents to $1.25.

Their soft drinks are carbonated natural drinks like ginger-lemon. And surprise, they have an interesting wine list personally picked from California, available by half liter or glass.

Reservations suggested for dinner.

The Brewery

Address: The Galleria, 122 North Street, Pittsfield, Mass., 01201.

Innkeepers: Susan and John Burke

Open: Lunch Monday-Saturday

This delightful luncheon room on the mezzanine of a downtown gallery of boutiques started out as a coffee shop in

1976 and just grew from there. If you come at noon on a week-day, you may have to wait in line.

Susan and John Burke, a young couple who hail from Philadelphia, operate the establishment with a crew of young people you'll find friendly and informal. Plants hang from the ceiling over butcherblock tables and big windows look out over Pittsfield's main shopping street.

The menu here is small, mostly soups, salads, and desserts, but the combinations are unusual and everything is scrumptious. Try the cucumber dill, or cold apple soups, or the hearty minestrone or seafood chowder. All are homemade. The fruit and vegetable salads are fresh and substantial. If you feel like nibbling, order a cheese board and if you just want dessert, the pastries are heaven-ly. Our favorite is the apple raisin cake.

Two can eat here for about $5.

British Maid

Address: Route 2, Williamstown, Mass., 01267, 413-458-4961

Open: Lunch, brunch, dinner, Tuesday-Saturday 7:30-2 p.m., 6-10 p.m.; Sunday brunch 8 a.m.-1 p.m. Closed Mondays. Entertainment weekends, bar, lounge, patio

The British Maid gets its name from Penelope Corbin who runs it with her family. Mrs. Corbin is British by birth, if you can't guess from the teatowels, homemade breakfast marmalade or British gourmet shop inside.

The Maid has grown like Topsey in recent years from a popular little breakfast restaurant to one of the most popular gathering places in town for lunch, brunch or evening drinks.

In summer, the cast from the Williamstown Theatre Festival are frequent habitues.

The cooking is what Mrs. Corbin likes to call "English country house cooking," but it's the crepes, omelettes and yummy desserts that make this a very popular spa for the Yankees.

Crepes average $4.50 for seafood, vegetable, chicken or cheese. You get two, but you can ask for only a half order. There are sandwiches, delicious chef's salads, all local produce in season, good soups, homemade breads, popovers, and desserts like English trifle, lemon or lime meringue pies, strawberry-rhubarb pie. With a little notice you can even order them to go and take home a treat.

For Sunday brunch, fill up on fresh squeezed fruit juice,

The British Maid, Williamstown, Credit: Stephanie L. Johnson

banana milk, fresh fruit bowls with cream, eggs Benedict, omelettes. Crepes are, alas, never offered on Sundays... its too crowded to cope.

The Maid is not a fast food place. Everything is cooked to order. It's not a good idea to expect to eat and run here.

Evening dinners feature lamb, veal, fresh fish dishes, mussels and escargots, with average entrees $7.

In summer, outside patio lunches under umbrellas, always a wine list, alcoholic license.

Reservations recommended.

Old English type bar and lounge upstairs, entertainment weekends, small groups, folk singers, vocalists, cover charge.

Ganesh Cafe

Address: 90 Church Street, Lenox, Mass., 01240, 413-637-1823

Open: Lunch and dinner specials. Sunday brunch from 9:00 a.m. Open daily noon to 11 p.m. Closed Tuesday. Open weekends in winter.

Ganesh is the very popular and corpulent god of good fortune and well being in India.

You'll find his likeness standing guard over the entrance to this witty outdoor cafe, garden and adjacent art gallery.

He is represented in Indian art and mythology with the head of a white elephant, a pot belly and the hand gesture signifying protective blessing. His name means god of the people in Sanskrit, and he is an epicure and a connoisseur in the art of selective eating. He also busies himself as the remover of obstacles invoked at the beginning of all important undertakings.

Probably for all of the above reasons, Honey Sharp, owner of the cafe and gallery which opened last summer, chose to have the little sphinx outside.

Purists who note this is in an historic district of town aren't too thrilled by his likeness, but everyone who eats here seems in agreement it is a delightful, affordable respite from the rich expensive meals offered in Lenox.

Vegetarians and those who make a point of searching out light homemade food will like the Tabbouleh, spinach, and chef's own garden tossed salads. The aqua minerale and cranberry juice crowd are ecstatic.

For Sunday brunch you will find fresh squeezed orange juice, begals from Brooklyn, New England apple fritters, the usual scramble of eggs with sausage, and toast for $3.75 and up.

At lunch there are salads, quiches, sandwiches, 10 omelettes, eight kinds of coffee, 10 varieties of tea, and always changing desserts for an average entree price of $2.75.

We picked a cold tomato and cucumber soup blended with yogurt. It was delicious. The chicken salad with walnuts, and a taste of a friend's quiche were also tasty.

Dinner specials may be Rock Cornish Game Hen with wild rice and side salad, or vegetarian stuffed zucchini for $6.75. The menu varies daily, fowl, fish, meat or vegetable.

In winter you eat inside where there are tables for a half dozen. Reservations are advised.

In summer you dine outside on the terrace. No reservations needed. Just scramble for your place in the sun.

La Cochina

Address: 140 Wahconah Street, Pittsfield, Mass., 01201, 413-499-4027

Innkeepers: Tom Borden and Gary Dubois

Open: Lunch and dinner. Open Monday through Saturday, 11 a.m. to 11 p.m.; Sunday, 1 to 10 p.m. Entertainment

La Cochina, which means "the kitchen" in Spanish, is not much to look at from the outside. It's not much on the inside either, with its checked tablecloths, mismatched chairs and straw donkey decorations. The food is what people come here for; honest-to-goodness Mexican dishes cooked light and savory for newcomers to this kind of cuisine, fiery hot for true connoisseurs.

Owners Tom Borden and Gary Dubois, who are brothers-in-law and Pittsfield natives, make everything to order and the menu cautions a 30-minute wait. It's time well invested.

We sampled nopalitos, strips of cactus with a faint, nutty taste and a texture like cooked peppers. The rancho, a house name for tortillas, stuffed with cheese and mushrooms and smothered in enchilada sauce, was light as a crepe and hot enough to leave a tingle in the mouth. For dessert, we tried sopapillas, light, fragrant puffs of dough, deep-fried and dipped in buckwheat honey.

The dinner menu features five different kinds of enchiladas as well as tacos, burritos and fish, chicken and pork dishes, all under $5. The bar lists a dozen Mexican specials in addition to beer and wine.

There's guitar entertainment most evenings.

Miss Ruby's Cafe

Address: Main Street, West Stockbridge, Mass., 01266, 413-232-8582

Open: Lunch and dinner, seven days a week. Brunch only Sunday. Dinner from 6-9:30 p.m. off season weekdays, 10 p.m. weekends. Summer, dinner till 10 p.m., midnight Friday and Saturday

Something is always cooking at Miss Ruby's and you won't know from one week to the next what it will be unless you call in advance. Try one Wednesday and the menu is Provencal. Try the next and the kitchen is turning out dishes from the Deep South. You take your chances here, but that's part of the fun of this place and of the woman who runs it, Ruth Adams Bronz, a Texas transplant who just loves to cook.

To eat at Miss Ruby's is to eat in a crazy kitchen where none of the furniture matches, the walls are painted purple and campy posters stare down at you while you dine. Waitresses chalk up menu changes on blackboards while running back and forth to the oven and serving counters, all out in plain view.

And if you think this is a place for just the blue jeans and sandals crowd, try to get in for Sunday brunch, as we did, and look at all the New York and Connecticut license plates bumper to bumper at the door.

Miss Ruby (or Ms. Bronz, if you prefer) believes there's a similarity to peasant cooking the world over. And this is the kind of cuisine she prepares: hearty, savory and imaginative. You'll find thick chowders, and gumbo, jambalaya, moussaka, along with Texas chili, lemon chicken, Mexican, soul food, light French vegetarian and hearty country stews.

Appetizers and soups begin at $1.50. The average price for entrees is $4.95.

We found the gazpacho soup garden fresh, thick with tomatoes and crisp peppers. The baba ganoush, a dip eaten with Syrian bread, was light and non-oily, and the carrot cake was rich and heavenly. That may sound like a peculiar dinner order, but that's the charm of this place, — it invites pure whimsey.

Her desserts are something else, rich concoctions like fudge pecan pie, and Junior League Fudge Cake which Miss Ruby says cheerfully would be a brownie except that it's much richer. You could just have plates of desserts here. And piles of fun.

Stockpot

Address: Pine Street, Stockbridge, Mass., 01262, 413-298-3592

Open: Breakfast Sunday. Lunch daily 9:30 a.m.-5 p.m. weekends till 9:30 p.m. for dinner. Tea or cocktails with canapes, hors d'ouevres, soups and quiches 3-5 p.m.

It looks like a Mom's apple pie type kitchen and it is. The Stockpot was originally built around 1850 by a cabinet maker. Since then it's been a home and furniture business, a wagon shop, blacksmith shop, home of a local druggist and dentist until evolving to its present occupation in 1972.

Real butter, fresh ground spices, homemade soups and pies, blended fresh roasted coffees with heavy country cream account for its homey feeling.

Generous sandwiches like the Stockpot Sovereign, a blend of turkey breast and ham on wheat toast with Swiss cheese, grilled tomatoes and pickles for $4.75 was our idea of the king pin sandwich. Reuben and open faced Danish sandwiches, fresh green salads, two quiches, a classic and a tasty Greek Spinach at $2.50, soups by cup or bowl, are also offered.

Desserts baked in the kitchen include cheesecake, butter cake, sour cream coffee cake and fruit pies a la mode, including, of course, apple, about $1.50.

Wine, beer, spirits are available.

Friday and Saturday evening dinners aren't fancy, but they are hearty; casseroles and stews.

Blended coffees and other goodies for sale in the adjoining small gourmet shop are fun to peruse after you pay your bill.

The Restaurant

Address: 15 Franklin Street, Lenox, Mass., 01240, 413-637-9894

Open: Brunch. Lunch, noon-2:30, Monday-Saturday; dinner, daily and Sunday from 6 p.m. Closed Wednesday

The Restaurant is an unassuming little place, paneled with barnboard, that serves, as they call it, "affectionately prepared meals."

The populace has responded in kind by favoring both the price, which is modest, and the choice, which runs an eclectic gamut, and has a lot of goodies for vegetarians.

Luncheon includes crepes, vegetable curry, sandwiches, chili con carne, knockwurst with sauerkraut, broiled turbot, $1.65 to $4.10, most in the $2 bracket.

Fresh squeezed orange juice at brunch; eggs, any style, $1.20; omelettes, $1.10, plus ingredients; French toast, $1.50; fruit pancakes, $2; crepes, $1.50 up.

Dinner begins at $2.65; tops $7.85 for marinated tenderloin steak. A la carte entrees include small salad, rice or vermicelli, fresh baked bread and butter.

Appetizers include buttered kippered herring in sauterne, fried banana, homos, pate maison, plum chutney. Entrees, which run the gamut from shrimp de jonghe to pork schnitzel with sauce choron, veal sweet breads bordelaise, eggplant and tomato pie, make this a place where the expertise in the kitchen is as erratic as the menu.

Basically it is an adventure. Take your chances. You'll find something to your taste and pocketbook.

Various coffees, teas, cider, spiced mocha, lemonade, or maybe a bloody Mary, fresh orange juice screwdriver, or glass of domestic house wine will wet your palate.

Desserts are a homemade potpourri of crepes, 80 cents to $1.25; bittersweet chocolate pudding, 60 cents; Arabian pudding, tapioca, lots of fresh fruits, fruitcake Alaska for two, delicious Angelica, a frozen whipped cream with almonds.

Railroad Street

Address: 20 Railroad Street, Great Barrington, Mass., 01230, 413-528-9345

Open: Lunch, Monday-Saturday, 11:30. Brunch, noon-2 p.m. Supper, Thursday only, 5:30-9 p.m.

A bar-and-brew place with a turn of the century feeling, this little establishment has both atmosphere and good soups, sandwiches and assorted burgers ranging in price from $1.25-$3.25.

Railroad Street, where this restaurant is located, got its name because of the proximity of the Housatonic Railroad tracks.

The massive mahogany bar which dominates the inside of this restaurant was built in New York City in 1883 and moved to town at the turn of the century. Twenty-eight feet long and brass fitted, it is called "mahogany ridge" by the locals who used to tell their wives tall tales during hunting season. Many an elbow and yarn were bent here.

Nowadays number 20 Railroad Street is a popular whistle stop for the younger set who queue up for lunch or Sunday brunch.

For brunch you can choose from eggs Benedict, quiche, French toast Monte Cristo or eggs any style served with bacon and sausage, home fries, fruit and a free drink (after noon), and coffee, all for $3.95. Children under 12 pay $1.75.

On Thursday, Italian dinners are the featured choice and there are three entrees to choose from. Entree, including salad, garlic breads, dessert and coffee, is $3.95 complete.

MUSEUMS

Berkshire Museum

Address: 39 South Street, Pittsfield, Mass., 01201

Days and
Hours Open: Tuesday through Saturday, 10 to 5; Sundays 2
to 5. Closed Mondays

Admission: Free

The Berkshire Museum has a little bit of everything inside its
walls, from modern art and photography, to English portraits,

Berkshire Museum, Pittsfield. Credit: Lewis C. Cuyler

stuffed animals, an Egyptian mummy and an automobile engine. And for its size, the quality and scope of its collections are surprisingly good.

The museum is small enough to tour in about an hour and the collections are grouped by subject so it's easy to find your way around. Science exhibits, including ones on Berkshire animals, birds, plants and geology are on the first floor, paintings and sculpture on the second.

While you're here, don't miss the local history room in the basement. For a 25-cent donation to the museum the guard will be happy to show it to you and wait while you browse. You'll find photographs of Pittsfield as it looked in the 19th century, including one of the Congregational Church designed by Charles Bulfinch that used to stand across the street from the museum until it was razed in 1936. Nathaniel Hawthorne's writing desk is here, as are examples of the guns and tools made in the area years ago. You'll also find "The Wonderful One-Horse Shay," which inspired the poem by Oliver Wendell Holmes, who summered here.

Sterling and Francine Clark Art Institute

Address: South Street, Williamstown, Mass., 01267

Days and

Hours Open: 10 to 5 p.m. Tuesday through Sunday. Closed Monday

Admission: Free

"The Clark," as it's known locally, is one of the Berkshires' cultural treasures and a must for any art lover visiting the area.

Built and endowed by Singer Sewing Machine heir Robert Sterling Clark and his French-born wife, Francine, the institute houses an exceptional collection of early French Impressionist paintings, 30 by Renoir, Monet, Degas as well as works by Corot, Sargent, Homer and Remington. Also a fine collection of English and American silver and French furniture.

The Clarks assembled most of their collection while living in Europe and moved it to the United States at the outbreak of World War II. They were persuaded to bring it to Williamstown, rather than New York City, by Professor Karl E. Weston, chairman emeritus of the Williams College art department, who was an old family friend and art advisor.

Mr. Clark, who died in 1956, personally supervised construction of the white marble building that still houses most of the collection, and the Clarks maintained a personal apartment at

Clark Art Institute, Williamstown, Credit: Stephanie L. Johnson

the museum which opened formally in 1955.

A new, granite addition with exhibition halls, theater and library for the Williams College graduate art program, designed by Pietro Belluschi of The Architects Collaborative in Boston, opened in 1973.

Since then the Clark has aggressively expanded its public offerings with numerous weekend concerts, lectures, readings, film festivals and retrospectives, as well as special on-loan exhibitions.

In summer the Clark and Williamstown Theatre Festival sponsor special Sundays at the Clark, events involving well known actors and actresses. In winter there is the Marlboro Music series.

Schedules of events are available or you may call for information.

Crane Museum

Address: Route 9, Dalton, Mass., 01226

Days and

Hours Open: Monday-Friday, 2 to 5. June-September

Admission: Free

The Crane Paper Co. mills are no longer open for public tours for security and safety reasons (Crane makes all the paper on which U.S. currency is printed), but the Crane Museum, established in 1929 and supported by the company, will show you just about everything you need to know about the history of papermaking.

This is a small museum, really only one room, made out of a portion of an early mill torn down near the beginning of the century. But it has been exquisitely restored and crafted and stands in a small graden near the company office. It takes some perseverence to find it and to know where to park your car, but don't give up.

If once inside you detect a slightly nautical atmosphere, there's a reason for it. Our interpreter, Harry P. Steadman, who will explain all the exhibits to you, told us a number of early mills had roofs designed along shipbuilding principles in order to span the work space below without using columns. The museum's roof, he said, is, in a sense, a ship's bottom turned upside down.

The exhibits, mostly scale models, photographs and paper samples, show you how paper is made from rags that are soaked, softened, beaten to pulp and dried. Crane uses only rags, no wood pulp, in its papermaking process, and its products are considered among the finest in the world.

You will learn how watermarks are made, how papers are finished hard or soft for different purposes and how currency papers are designed to discourage counterfeiting. And you will see historic documents, White House invitations and U.S. and foreign money, all printed on Crane paper.

At the end of the visit, each adult who signs the guest book gets a free envelope of Crane paper samples.

The Old Corner House

Address: Main Street, Stockbridge, Mass., 01262

Days and

Hours Open: Daily 10 to 5 p.m. Closed Tuesday, Thanksgiving, Christmas and New Year's Day

Admission: Adults, $1, children under 12, 25 cents

The Old Corner House has the only permanent collection of Norman Rockwell paintings on public exhibit in the United States, including many familiar Saturday Evening Post covers.

Rockwell lived from 1953 until the fall of 1978, when he died, as a familiar resident of this small town. His studio is only two blocks away.

There are about 65 paintings normally hanging at any one time, among them Rockwell's famous "Self Portrait," which shows him humorously looking at himself painting himself. There is also the famous "Four Freedoms" cover of 1941. Locals can recognize themselves in his works, they were often the models. His painting of the village Main Street hangs inside, the real thing is right outside for comparison.

The collection is shown by guided tour only and the house is apt to be crowded as all of Stockbridge is in summer when the population literally swells to double. The best time to visit is an off-peak day.

Paintings here are not for sale, but you may buy books and prints, post cards and calendars in the gift gallery, and on occasion limited edition signed lithographs.

The Old Corner House itself is a handsome Georgian residence built in the late 18th century and acquired in 1967 by a local citizens group who formed a corporation to preserve and maintain it as a museum. The Stockbridge Historical Society also has its collections on exhibit here.

The house was the one-time home of author Rachel Field who wrote the children's classic, "Hitty: Her First Hundred Years," and "All This and Heaven Too."

Albert Schweitzer Friendship House and Library

Address: Hurlburt Road, Great Barrington, Mass., 01230, 413-528-3124

Days and
Hours Open: By appointment, but don't worry. They're not stuffy here. Just call to verify hours open.

If you ask what connection the legendary humanitarian Albert Schweitzer had with the Berkshires, the answer is none, directly. But he so inspired filmmaker Erica Anderson, who met him for the first time 20 years ago, that after his death in 1965 she set up this museum and library to commemorate and record his work.

Mrs. Anderson, who died in 1976, visited Schweitzer numerous times at his hospital in Lambarene, Gabon, Africa and took

Albert Schweitzer Friendship House, Great Barrington,
Credit: Stephanie L. Johnson

thousands of photographs as well as films, one of which received an Oscar in the documentary class.

Her work, as well as countless other papers, documents, photographs, and tapes have been assembled here to form one of the largest complete Schweitzer collections in this country. You can pore over 30,000 photographs mounted in loose-leaf volumes, read every book Schweitzer wrote, and hundreds written about him, or listen to taped conversations between Mrs. Anderson and Schweitzer, Albert Einstein and cellist Pablo Casals.

Mrs. Anderson set up Friendship House using $10,000 Schweitzer left to her when he died in thanks for her years of volunteer work with him. Impressed by the peace and beauty of the Berkshires, she bought this house and barn on 40 acres and over the years converted the barn into a library and theater with seating for 100. Films are shown at 2 p.m. Saturdays and Sundays in summer and special arrangements can be made for groups.

The Schweitzer house and library are set up as a nonprofit tax exempt educational organization supported by contributions and foundation support.

You can peruse the photographs at leisure, bring a lunch to eat outside on the patio picnic table, or amble through the small sanctuary in the woods out back where his words are etched in wood plaques and a stream runs peacably alongside.

It is an appropriate setting in which to ponder his simple humanitarian philosophy and reverence for life.

Williams College Museum of Art

Address: Route 2, just east of Spring Street, Williamstown, Mass., 01267

Days and
Hours Open: Daily, 10 to noon and 2 to 4; Sundays, 2 to 5. Closed July 4, Labor Day and college holidays

Admission: Free

As the name implies, this is a college art museum. And while it's small (you can tour it in about 20 minutes) the collection is a good one and exhibits change often. The permanent collection has some fine American, English and early Spanish furniture, but it's the temporary and loan exhibits we find most exciting. Many of them are arranged by graduate students in the Williams art department and, depending on when you go, you may find modern sculpture that moves or lights up, abstract painting and graphics or photos and maps of an archaeological dig in southern France.

The college museum, with its modern bent, complements the Sterling and Francine Clark Art Institute on South Street a few blocks away, which concentrates on the Impressionist era.

Col. John Ashley House

Address: Cooper Hill on Old Route 7, three-fourths mile west of Ashley Falls in Sheffield, Mass., 01257

*Days and
Hours Open:* Memorial Day Weekend through Columbus Day, Wednesday - Sunday, 1 - 5

Admission: Adults, $1.25; children 16 and under, 30 cents

If we tell you the Col. John Ashley House is the oldest in Berkshire County, which it is — built in 1735 — you might find that reason enough to take a side trip to visit it. But there's more. If you're a nature lover, you'll find it's linked to one of the best wildlife and plant preserves in the Berkshires, Bartholomew's Cobble. And if you're a real history buff, you'll discover it's tied to two important events in American history, separation from England and the freeing of the slaves.

For its age, the house is exquisitely preserved and this alone would make it special. You'll find the handsome interior paneling and even the plaster are original, thanks to the loving care the house was given by a descendent of Col. Ashley, who rescued it during the 1930s and kept it as a museum until it passed to the Massachusetts Trustees of Reservations, who now own and maintain it as well as nearby Bartholomew's Cobble.

Col. Ashley, who died in 1802 at the age of 93, was an officer in the French and Indian Wars, a founder of the Town of Sheffield and a leader in the movement to establish Berkshire County as a political entity.

It was here in his house in 1772 that the first declaration of independence from England was drafted. It was a local protest against English rule and was adopted at the Sheffield Town Meeting of January 12, 1773. It preceded by three years the national Declaration in Philadelphia.

Col. Ashley was also a figure, though in this case the villain, in another bid for independence that resulted in the abolition of slavery in Massachusetts.

He had, among the servants in his household, a black slave, Elizabeth Freeman, better known in history as "Mum Bett." She overheard the talk in the late 1760s about the new state constitution and its guarantees of freedom and equality for all. After an argument one day with Mrs. Ashley over some household matter, she fled to a neighbor, Theodore Sedgewick, and asked him to secure her freedom under the law. Although Sedgewick was a friend of Ashley's, he brought him to court and won. The decision abolished slavery in Massachusetts and made Mum Bett the first slave in America to win her freedom by legal suit.

Arrowhead

Address: 780 Holmes Road, Pittsfield, Mass., 01201

Days and
Hours Open: May 1 to October 31. Weekdays, 10 to 5 p.m.; Sundays 1 to 5 p.m. Closed Tuesdays

Admission: Adults $1; students, 50 cents

Herman Melville came to the Berkshires in 1850 a celebrity of sorts. His tales of the South Seas enjoyed a wide popular following.

But thirteen years later he left Arrowhead, his home, dispirited and sliding into debt. It was while he was here, however, that he wrote what has come to be regarded as his masterpiece, "Moby Dick."

No stranger to the Berkshires, he was born in New York and grew up around Albany, often summering in Pittsfield on his uncle's farm which is now the Pittsfield Country Club.

In later years he was drawn back again, craving a congenial place in which to write, a way to supplement his income by farming, and a peaceful rural environment for his family.

He found such a place at Arrowhead, which he named for the Indian artifacts he found in nearby fields. Arrowhead was built originally as a stagecoach inn in 1790. Melville was neither the first nor last to own it. He lived here just over a dozen years. While he was here Nathaniel Hawthorne, who became his close friend, was in residence six miles away in Lenox also writing what was to be "The House of Seven Gables," and Oliver Wendell Holmes was his neighbor a mile down the road. The Berkshires was enjoying popularity as a literary enclave.

Melville began Moby Dick in 1851 and for a few years, it seemed he'd found what he'd been searching for. The rural surroundings eased and inspired him, but once the book was completed life took a downward turn.

Moby Dick with its deep psychological probing of good and evil was not a book the American public accepted in its time. Its critical rejection was a crushing disappointment to its author as well as a financial disaster. Melville followed Moby Dick with a second novel, "Pierre," which raised the topic of sibling incest. It too fell on deaf ears.

Faced with mounting debts he began writing magazines articles and delivering lectures, finally disposing of Arrowhead in 1863 to take a $4 a day job as a customs inspector in New York. He died in 1891, obscure.

Arrowhead fared better by comparison, passing through several owners before the Berkshire County Historical Society bought it in 1975 and set to work restoring it to Melville's time. The piazza which inspired Melville's "Piazza Tales" has been restored, his study refurbished and filled with books he referred to in his writings, the house furnished with pieces appropriate to the period. Melville's own writing desk and memorabilia are housed in the Melville room at the Berkshire Athenaeum. But here you can see the kitchen fireplace which inspired his short story, "I and My Chimney" as it was when Melville scribbled and etched on its stone. The barn, where he and Hawthorne spent hours discussing their work, has likewise been restored.

The original farm has, with time, dwindled down from 160 acres to less than 15 now, but the house framed by giant elms and pines, surrounded by quiet and open fields remains a quiet peaceful reminder of Melville's days spent here in what was perhaps the happiest period of his life.

Chesterwood

Address: Off Route 183, two miles north of Route 102, Stockbridge, Mass., 01262

Days and
Hours Open: Daily, 10 to 5, from May 1 to October 31
Admission: $2 adults, $1 children, students, elders

"I spend six months of the year here. That is heaven," sculptor Daniel Chester French once said of his Berkshire estate, Chesterwood. "New York is — well, New York."

And if you happen to come here on a quiet late-spring day as we did, and gaze out across the soft lawns to the Housatonic River and Monument Mountain in the distance, you may just agree that this could be a bit like paradise.

French, who is best known for his Seated Lincoln statue in Washington, D.C. and for his Minute Man at Concord, Mass., was already a successful artist when he came to Stockbridge in 1896 and purchased a 120-acre farm to use as a summer home. Two years later he began building a studio, choosing as his architect his friend Henry Bacon, who later designed the Lincoln Memorial and secured for French the commission for the Lincoln statue.

What Bacon created at Chesterwood, with French's collaboration, was an airy, luxurious working space, as much a salon as a studio, with a living area, fireplace and library for entertaining, a terraced garden adorned by a fountain for viewing and a sweeping piazza overlooking the valley to relax upon.

To accommodate the massive sculptures for which French was famous, Bacon made the studio ceilings 23 feet high and even installed a railroad track so works in progress could be moved outside, on a rolling platform, and studied in the sunlight.

Exactingly planned for its special function, the studio was French's world for more than three decades. It was here that he planned and executed the Lincoln statue, entertained his visitors and relaxed in a hammock on the piazza, gazing over the Berkshire hills he loved.

The two-story, Georgian style mansion on the grounds, also designed by Bacon, was built in 1900 to replace the original farmhouse. French's office, to the right of the front door, contains the panels, lintels and mantle from the original dwelling and the sitting room is a recreation of one in the French family homestead in Chester, N.H.

French died in 1931, leaving the estate to his daughter, Margaret French Cresson, who donated it to the National Trust for Historic Preservation in 1969. It is a National Historic Landmark and Massachusetts Historic Landmark.

The sculptor's tools, plaster casts, notebooks and drawings are exhibited in the studio and in a barn nearby that's been converted into a gallery and museum shop. Visitors are welcome to try their hands at clay modelling in the Guest Sculpture area and to amble the nature trails French laid out in the forest north of his studio.

Hancock Shaker Village

Address: Intersection of Routes 20 and 41, Hancock, Mass., 01237

Days and
Hours Open: Daily, 9:30 a.m. to 5 p.m. June to November
Admission: $3.50 adults, $1 children

Once an important Shaker settlement and now a museum village with 18 of its 22 buildings carefully restored, Hancock Shaker Village is an experience you will want to save a full afternoon, or better yet, a day to enjoy.

There are no guides here to hurry you along, no set paths to follow. Simply amble at your leisure from exhibit to exhibit, spending as much or as little time as you please. Everything is

The round Stone Barn, Hancock Shaker Village, Hancock,
Credit: Stephanie L. Johnson

clearly explained on plaques and cards at each building.

The Shakers, as you'll see, believed that form follows function. They were an inventive people constantly seeking more efficient ways of doing things. They developed the box stove in 1810 to replace heat-wasting open fireplaces, the flat broom and the ladderback chair. The buildings they designed were light and airy with lots of built-in cupboards to eliminate dust-catching corners and wall pegs to hang unneeded chairs and stools out of the way.

The buildings at Hancock Shaker Village exhibit this kind of inventiveness everywhere: in the living quarters, kitchens, working rooms; in the furnishings, clothing and everyday articles arranged casually as though the occupants had just for a moment stepped away.

The round Stone Barn, for instance, probably the most impor-

Making pitchforks, Hancock Shaker Village, Hancock,
Credit: Stephanie L. Johnson

tant building here architecturally, allowed one man to feed an entire herd of cattle at once, each animal facing inward in a circle of stanchions.

The Shakers themselves, unfortunately for them, were not as inventive or forward thinking about their future. A religious sect, founded by Mother Ann Lee in the 18th century, they believed in a highly ordered communal, but celibate, life and service to God. They came to the United States from England in 1774 and established 19 settlements in New England, New York, Ohio, Indiana and Kentucky. Living apart from, but trading freely with, outside society they grew rich and earned respect for their ingenuity and business acumen.

But they failed to attract continual converts and by the 20th century their movement was at a standstill. Today fewer than a

Carving a tombstone, Hancock Shaker Village, Hancock,
Credit: Stephanie L. Johnson

dozen Shakers are left, mostly in New Hampshire and Maine.

Hancock village itself was abandoned by its last inhabitants in the 1950s. Acquired in 1960 by a non profit organization, Shaker Village Inc., it was restored and opened as a museum.

The restoration kept an environment that would have pleased the Shakers themselves. You will find no guides dressed here in Shaker costumes, no animals to feed (although livestock are pastured nearby) no bumper stickers or pennants to promote the place. It is all tastefully done and meant to be a learning experience.

The visitors' center, where you come in, has a gift shop bookstore well stocked with Shaker history, philosophy, crafts and cooking.

A nearby lunch room-cafeteria offers soups, sandwiches, pie and ice cream. Try the Shakers' own rose geranium ice cream, a cool summer treat.

Just beyond the entry building is the herbal garden where the variety of herbs the Shakers were known to use for decorative, medicinal and cooking purposes grow in abundant, neatly groomed, fragrant rows.

The first week of August a kitchen festival gives samplers a taste of the Shakers' culinary craftsmanship, There are dinners, made up from Shaker recipes, and lots of available goodies fresh to buy.

In mid August, an annual crafts festival brings together a variety of craftsmen who give demonstrations daily on how the Shakers made their brooms, baskets, ironware and wove their cloth.

The beginning of October marks the Autumn Festival and a series of special demonstrations and events that pivot around an autumn harvest.

The Mission House

Address: Main Street, Stockbridge, Mass., 01262
Days and
Hours Open: May 28 to October 15, Tuesday - Saturday, 10 to 5; Sunday, 11 to 4.
Admission: $1.40 adults; under 14, 30 cents

The Mission House is as much the story of two people and the worlds they represented as it is a superb example of New England architecture that dates back to colonial times.

Weathered and stately with a Georgian facade and gardens fragrant with oleander, mint and lemon balm, it was built in 1739 by the Rev. John Sergeant, first missionary to the Stockbridge Indians, as a wedding gift to his bride, Abigail Williams, daughter of a powerful landowning family.

While Sergeant had been content before his marriage to live among the Indians he taught, his wife made it clear from the start she would not. To please her, he built this house on a site near that of her parents' home on what is now Prospect Hill. It was a gesture Sergeant could evidently ill-afford, for though he enjoyed a comfortable income during his life, when he died he was deeply in debt.

The Mission House allowed the Sergeants to live side by side, yet in separate worlds. The front of the house was Abigail's territory, the front parlors made extra large for entertaining by moving the chimneys back from the ridge line. The massive front door, the building's most striking feature, was carved in Westfield and dragged 50 miles over rugged terrain to

Stockbridge.

The back of the house was John Sergeant's realm. The small study he used was connected by a long corridor to a separate entrance so his Indian visitors would not have to pass through the rest of the house.

John Sergeant died in 1749 and with him the mission folded. By 1785, the Indians had been pushed out of Stockbridge by land speculators like Abigail's family. Descendents of the tribe now live in Wisconsin.

Abigail remarried after Sergeant's death. She died at the Mission House in 1791.

The house was acquired in 1927 by Mabel Choate, an art collector and philanthropist whose family built the Naumkeag estate in Stockbridge. She had the Mission House dismantled and moved to its present site where it has been restored, and gave it to the Trustees of Reservations who maintain it as a museum.

Few of the furnishings are original to the house, but all are authentic of the period and approximate the way things looked when John and Abigail lived there. Abigail's cookbook, her wedding slippers and John's study chair are here. The children's room is a special delight with its toys and dolls.

The gardens around the house were designed by Fletcher Steele, the Boston landscape architect who laid out Naumkeag's gardens. They are patterned after an 18th century model and make use of herbs and flowers that would have grown there in the Sergeants' time.

Naumkeag

Address: Prospect Hill (off Route 102), Stockbridge, Mass., 01262

Days and
Hours Open: Tuesday - Saturday 10-5, Sunday and holidays 11-4. Closed Mondays and in winter. Reopens weekends Memorial Day until June 23 then full schedule resumes. Weekends only again from Labor Day through Columbus Day.

Admission: House and garden tour, $2.25; house only, $1.60; garden, $1.10; children 6-12, 60 cents, under six free; group rates

"Naumkeag," an Indian word meaning haven of peace, was the summer home of Joseph H. Choate, lawyer for the Rockefeller family, and once ambassador to the Court of St. James.

The elegant, shingle-style mansion, designed by Stanford White in 1885, was used as a residence by the family for 71 years and was given in 1956 to the Trustees of Reservations, who now maintain it as a museum.

While Choate is always identified as the builder of Naumkeag, it was his daughter, Mabel, who inherited it, who fashioned the house and grounds into what they are today, a sumptuous environment, half fantasy and half country home, filled with oriental art, rich furnishings and lavish gardens.

An energetic, widely travelled woman, Miss Choate never married and devoted her life to philanthropic work, the collecting of art and the embellishment of Naumkeag. She spent years in the Orient, buying and sending home crates of Chinese sculpture, pottery, rugs and furniture, much of it displayed here along with fine English china, Waterford crystal chandeliers and family portraits by Sargent.

Fascinated by landscape architecture, Miss Choate transformed the rugged slopes and pastures surrounding the house into a private world of terraces and walkways, falling water and sculptured topiary. Step through a gate and you're in a Venetian garden, dark and cool, where water drips from a tiny fountain and gondola posts form a colonnade. Climb a hill and enter a door and you're in a Chinese temple, silent and serene, looking out over the distant mountains. Descend a staircase and you're in a grove of birch trees, water cascading beside the steps at your feet.

Naumkeag is a glimpse of the Berkshires as they were in a golden era of big estates, legendary names and vast fortunes. It is a world we will never see again.

Quaker Meeting House

Address: Maple Street, Adams, 01220
Days and
Hours Open: The building itself is closed to the public.

Built in 1782 by the Quakers who first settled this community, this simple, unpainted frame structure is probably the only

Quaker Meeting House, Adams, Credit: Lewis C. Cuyler

meeting house left of its age that's still close to its original condition.

It was used for about 60 years until the Quakers moved west to Farmington, N.Y. Susan B. Anthony, famed suffragette and Adams native, worshipped here.

The building has two doors and is divided by a moveable partition because the men and women worshipped separately and even kept separate records.

Each fall, the Society of Friends gather here for an annual worship service, which is open to the public. The building is owned by the Town of Adams and is a national historic site.

NATURAL BEAUTY

Bartholomew's Cobble

Address:	Follow signs on Route 7 through Sheffield, Mass., 01257
Days and Hours Open:	April 15 through October 15; Wednesday through Sunday, 9 to 5
Admission:	$1.25 adults; under 16, 30 cents

A limestone outcropping that rises above the Housatonic River, Bartholomew's Cobble is a natural rock garden lush with ferns that thrive on its lime-rich soil. It is one of the best fern habitats in New England, home to some of the rarest species of this plant form.

Walking its trails, you'll see how plants gradually convert rock to soil, how simple lichens and mosses build up a spongy seedbed on which more complex ferns and flowers, and later trees and shrubs can develop.

From the Cobble, you can see the Housatonic River meandering through the fertile farmland created by deposits of silt it's carried down from the uplands.

Hopkins Forest

Address:	Northwest Hill Road, Williamstown, Mass., 01267

This 1600-acre woodland laced with hiking and bridle trails was a working farm back in the early 19th century, its slopes cleared of trees and lined with stone walls.

Owned today by Williams College, which maintains it as a nature-studies area, it illustrates how a forest regenerates itself. Pick up one of the trail guides in the box beside the large map at the parking area. The numbers you'll see posted along the trails correspond to the descriptions in the guide of the stages of forest growth. If you're persevering, you may find the foundations of the old farmhouse built here years ago. The barn near the parking area was reconstructed from timbers dragged from the farmhouse site. It houses exhibits of 19th century farm tools.

Hopkins Forest is more an outdoor classroom than a recreation area. There are no picnic tables, snack bars or restrooms here. And if you're going to do any serious hiking, wear thick-soled shoes. The trails are laced with ground springs.

Hopkins Forest is popular with cross-country skiers in winter. It's opened by permit to local hunters the first week of December each year, and is best avoided at that time.

Bash Bish Falls

Address: Mount Washington

Though only 50 feet high, Bash Bish is the most spectacular falls in Berkshire County. After cutting through a rock gorge 400 feet high, Bash Bish Brook leaps over a precipice, sending up clouds of mist in which, it is said, one can sometimes see the profile of an Indian maiden who, disappointed in love, threw herself over the cliff far above. The falls plunge into a deep clear pool which empties toward Taconic State Park, across the New York line.

You can view the falls from a parking lot above and then climb the steep trail down to the plunge pool. To reach it, turn right off East Road at the church and town hall in Mount Washington and continue on Cross Road west toward New York State, following the signs for Bash Bish.

You can also reach the base of the falls on a foot trail from Taconic State Park, where you'll find parking and picnic areas.

Monument Mountain

Address: Great Barrington, Mass.

Monument Mountain, at 1750 feet, is probably the loveliest peak in the Berkshires. William Cullen Bryant wove a poem around it, Hudson River artist Asher Durand painted it, sculptor Daniel Chester French built a studio so he could look at it and Nathaniel Hawthorne wrote about it.

Sharp and craggy, its summit bare of vegetation, it rises from the Housatonic Valley floor like a monolith, its base draped in forest. The mountain was named for a monument of stones the Indians built nearby many years ago for reasons that have been lost in legend.

Much of the enchantment of Monument Mountain is that it is unspoiled. Take either of two trails to the top and you'll find no fire towers, lookout posts or concession stands, just beautiful views over the valley and the Housatonic River meandering far below. The sharp-eyed might spy the Great Barrington landfill east of the base, but it's a small scar on an otherwise gentle and peaceful landscape. In June, the laurel that grows on the mountain comes into bloom for a magnificent show.

Owned by the Trustees of Reservations, Monument Mountain is maintained as a public recreation area with trails for hiking, snowshoeing or cross country skiing. There are limited picnic facilities and no camping is allowed.

You'll find the parking area and trail entrance on Route 7 across from Monument Mountain Regional High School.

Mount Everett

Address: Mount Washington, Mass.

Second highest peak in the state at 2,624 feet, Mount Everett is a hikers' delight, laced with trails that skirt tumbling brooks and waterfalls, descend deep ravines and traverse rocky bluffs. From the fire tower at the summit, you can look out over four states: Massachusetts, Connecticut, Vermont and New York.

Easiest walk to the top, about 2.5 miles, is along the Elbow Trail, which starts on the campus of the Berkshire School off Route 41 in Sheffield. Steepest and most spectacular is the Race Brook Trail, which will take you past a series of waterfalls, one of them more than 100 feet high. It begins at a rest area on the west side of Route 41 south of the Berkshire School.

If you're not up to climbing the whole way to the summit, you can drive to within a few hundred yards of it on a well-marked road off East Road, the main north-south highway in Mount Washington. The road will take you to a large parking and picnic area adjacent to Guilder Pond then up to a lookout area with views of the Housatonic Valley toward Litchfield, Conn. From there, you can walk up the rest of the way, it takes about 15 minutes. Or, starting at Guilder Pond, you can take a portion of the Appalachian Trail to the top. The trail enters the Mount Everett Reservation near Jug End resort in Egremont and continues along a ridge south of Mount Everett toward Connecticut.

If you are hiking the Appalachian Trail you will find good views along this ridge, and if you want to test yourself on the challenging Race Brook Trail, it intersects the Appalachian here.

If you visit the mountain in midsummer, keep an eye out for wild blueberries that grow along the trails.

Maps and information are available from state employees at the reservation.

Mount Greylock

Address: Adams (Visitors' Center, Rockwell Road, Lanesboro) or via Notch Road, Route 2, North Adams, Mass., 01247.

Days and
Hours Open: Memorial Day until Columbus Day. Closed in winter

War Memorial Tower, Mount Greylock, Adams,
Credit: Lewis C. Cuyler

Mount Greylock, 3,491 feet above sea level, is the highest point in Massachusetts. On a clear day the views from its summit extend all the way to Connecticut, New York and Vermont. The Berkshires are spread out below this giant like a green carpet, studded with lakes; the town of Adams, like a tiny toy village. Because you are above the tree line in what is actually a tundra environment, there is no foliage to block the dramatic panorama.

You can drive to the top on paved roads from two directions. Rockwell Road off Route 7 in Lanesboro (well-marked with signs, just past the Old Stone Church heading north) is about 15 miles long and fairly easy driving. At the Visitors' Center, about two miles up, you'll find pamphlets, maps and guides to places to camp and hike on the reservation. The Notch Road, about two miles west of North Adams on Route 2, is shorter, nine miles, but more winding route to the top. The sharp drop-offs and dramatic views reward the adventuresome.

The War Memorial Tower with its beacon light, built in the 1930s and rebuilt in the 1970s, crowns the summit. There is ample parking, and a restaurant and inexpensive dormitory-type accommodations are at Bascom Lodge near the tower; $6 per person in shared rooms of two to six people, $3 with your own sleeping bag.

Greylock is especially popular during the fall foliage season, and when the colors are at their peak, around Columbus Day weekend, the cars and buses are lined bumper to bumper near the top.

The weather is fierce at the summit in winter (see what it did to the flag now displayed inside Bascom Lodge), so the road to the summit is closed all winter.

Natural Bridge

Address: Route 8, North Adams, Mass., 01247
Days and
Hours Open: Daily until October
Admission: $1

The only natural marble bridge in North America, estimated to be 550 million years old or about 150 million years older than the formation of Niagara Falls, it is owned and presided over by Eddie Elder who bought the bridge in 1950.

His brochure and speeches about the site alone are worth the admission.

Only an almanac could surpass the brochure for sheer number of facts packed into limited space.

At first glance you will see a semi-circle of quarried marble wall, footpath, chain-link fence and sturdy wooden platforms to the bridge itself. Mr. Elder likens these quarry walls to "the pages of God's history written when the world was younger and man was not here to write about it."

Mr. Elder bought the bridge several years after the last mining company had finished extracting the marble from a nearby quarry. He's found graffiti that dates back to 1837 carved in the rock which is 1,100 feet above sea level resting now on marine deposits placed here by nature millions of years ago when this part of the world was under water.

But perhaps Nathaniel Hawthorne gives the finest description: "It is like a heart that has been rent asunder by a torrent of passion, which has raged and roared, and left its ineffaceable traces; though now there is but a little rill of feeling at the bottom."

Notchview

Address:	Route 9, Windsor, Mass., 01270
Days and Hours Open:	Year round until dusk. Visitors' Center, Friday, Saturday, Sunday and holidays, 10 to 4
Admission:	50 cents; children 14 and under, free

A 3,000 acre spruce and hardwood forest that sprawls over the Windsor plateau, Notchview was once a huge estate and, before that, a settlement of some two dozen farms. It is owned today by the Massachusetts Trustees of Reservations who maintain it as a forest-management and passive-recreation area.

Notchview, like Hopkins Forest in Williamstown, illustrates how human settlements are reclaimed by forests once man abandons his farming and lumbering activities. This kind of reclamation began in many parts of the Berkshires when early settlers left their homesteads here in the mid 19th century for better land in the Midwest.

Notchview is laced with 25 miles of hiking trails, including an interpretive trail near Hume Brook that explains the principles of forest management. You can hike or picnic in summer, follow the trails on snowshoes or cross-country skis in winter. You'll find evidence of the original farms in stone walls and old foundations.

Trail guides, at 20 cents each, are tucked into the box below the large map at the parking area. You are on your honor to pay for them, as well as the small entry fee, when the visitors' center is not open.

Pleasant Valley Wildlife Sanctuary

Address:	Off Route 7 opposite Holiday Inn between Lenox and Pittsfield, Mass., 413-637-0320
Hours Open:	Daily, sunrise to sunset
Admission:	$1 adults, 50 cents students. Audubon members free. No dogs allowed

The 680 acres here at the base of Lenox Mountain are made up of meadows, swamps, and forests maintained by the Massachusetts Audubon Society.

The sanctuary has seven and a half miles of trails for nature walks and cross country skiing in winter.

There is a small trailside museum and live exhibits of native plants, fish, snakes and other animals. The museum is open daily after Memorial Day 10-4:30 P.M., weekends only in spring and fall.

Guided walking tours and educational experiences are planned on a scheduled basis.

A private gift of land to the Audubon Society to establish a wildlife refuge, it is teeming with flora and fauna, and yet peacefully serene at the same time.

Pleasant Valley lives up to its name.

One of the most popular animal habitats is that of the beavers which were reintroduced here in 1932 and have since thrived. You can see evidence of their architecture and learn how they affect the ecological landscape, but don't be disappointed if you don't catch a glimpse of them.

Windsor Jambs

Address: Windsor State Forest, River Road, Windsor, Mass., 01270

Days and
Hours Open: May 1 through October 15

Cut by a brook that flows out of Windsor Pond, the Jambs is a deep, narrow gorge with almost vertical walls (hence its name) that wends through a fragrant pine forest. You can follow a roped walk from the parking area for about a quarter of a mile along the top of the chasm and peer down at the rushing water and cataracts below. The walk ends in a series of pools you can explore if you're adept and sure-footed.

On the main road, at the turn-off to the Jambs, a handsome, state-run recreation area has been developed for picnicking and swimming. A dam, with a spillway, backs up a brook-fed reservoir ringed with grassy areas and a small, sandy beach. There's a 24-site camping area nearby as well as hiking and bridle trails. Ask at the office near the main parking area.

Berkshire Theatre Festival

Address:	Berkshire Playhouse, East Main Street, Stockbridge, Mass., 01262. 413-298-5576 or Chargit 800-223-0120
Open:	June 28 - August 27
Main Stage:	Performances Wednesday-Friday 8:30 p.m., Saturday 5 p.m. and 9 p.m., Sunday 7:30 p.m. Matinees Thursday and Sunday
Tickets:	$5 - $9.95; may be charged by phone with major credit cards

Berkshire Playhouse, Stockbridge, Credit: Stephanie L. Johnson

The second oldest summer theater in the United States operates three performance facilities on its eight acre grounds: The Berkshire Playhouse, the Unicorn Theater and the Proposition Workshop.

The Berkshire Playhouse, designed as the Stockbridge Casino in 1886 by Stanford White, was the social center of Stockbridge until the mid 1920's. Plays, art exhibits, lectures and dances were given here.

Originally located on Main Street where the Mission House now is, it was moved to the present location on Yale Hill in 1928. It is listed in the National Registry of Historic Places.

Famous names that have been associated with the Playhouse include Katharine Hepburn, James Cagney, Montgomery Clift, Tallulah Bankhead, Ethel Barrymore, Estelle Parsons and Anne Bancroft. Thornton Wilder and William Gibson were playwrights intimately involved with the Playhouse. More recently Eva Marie Saint, and in 1978, Joanne Woodward performed here.

For the last ten years the main stage has concentrated on American theater, either revivals of classic American plays, or new and experimental works.

The Proposition Workshop, a young five year old company founded in Cambridge, Mass., presents theater of a different style than the main stage productions. A core company of some 25 actors, structured like a choreographer's company, take turns acting on a minimally propped stage. The shows they put on may be documentary, or historical in essence drawing their materials from letters, diaries, or oral histories put to or without music.

The other small theater, the Unicorn Theater, also does experimental theater. Very often there are special plays for children.

Jacob's Pillow Dance Festival

Address:	George Carter Road, Becket, Mass., 01223
Open:	July 1 - August 26
Performances:	Tuesday - Saturday evenings; Saturday matinees
Tickets:	$6 - $8 at box office, Ticketron, Chargit. Must be purchased in advance

If you love dance, this festival offers outstanding examples of every form.

Classical ballet is represented as are works by major choreographers and innovative new trend setters.

Pilobolus, Paul Taylor, Alvin Ailey, the Boston Ballet, Berkshire Ballet, Charles Moore and Dances and Drums of

Africa, Los Indianos are equally at home here.

The Pillow was a rundown 18th century barn on 150 acres when it was bought by choreographer Ted Shawn in 1931. Two years later he formed an all male dance company which challenged all stereotypes of men dancing and toured every state in the country. Summer performances and lectures grew into the Jacob's Pillow Dance Festival and the University of Dance at the Pillow.

Now entering its 47th season, dance here has become the realization of Ted Shawn's dream. Shared by men and women alike, dance is a soaring art that speaks a universal language.

Shakespeare & Co.

Address:	The Mount, Plunkett Road, Lenox, Mass., 01240, 413-637-1197
Open:	July - Labor Day
Performances:	Weekend evenings on the grounds
Tickets:	$5

This is a brand new company of classical Shakespearean actors headed by artistic director Tina Packer, a Britisher with an atypical approach to the classics.

They moved — lock, stock and barrel, scrub brush and manuscript — into what was once Edith Wharton's Berkshire summer place and in one summer (1978) captured the delight of audiences with their magical performances of "A Midsummer Night's Dream."

The sets were natural — the forest, lawn, back balconies of the house — but it was the language that glistened, spoken by actors whose musical poetry has to be heard to be believed.

We don't know what they will be up to when you read this, but they plan to buy the house and give both it and Shakespeare renewed breath.

We think Edith Wharton would be simply delighted if she knew who was dusting out her attic.

The house itself was modeled by Mrs. Wharton after one by Christopher Wren in Lincolnshire, England. It is spacious, elegant, a neo-Georgian beauty that passed through various owners and was most recently a girls school. Neglected, it fell into disrepair. This company intends with time to restore it and the grounds while they live in, and give out, Shakespearean classics.

The Mount, former home of Edith Wharton, Lenox,
Credit: Stephanie L. Johnson

South Mountain Concerts

Address: Routes 7 and 20, one mile south of Pit-
                               tsfield, Mass., 01201, 413-442-0130
Open: June - October
Performances: Saturday, 3 p.m. June, July and
                               August; Sundays in September and
                               October
Tickets: $6 - $9

For over 60 years South Mountain has been one of America's most distinguished musical centers.

It was founded in 1918 by Mrs. Elizabeth Sprague Coolidge, who was "a fairy godmother to chamber music". She built a summer home, concert hall and several musicians' cottages on the wooded slopes of her property and founded the Pittsfield chamber music festival.

Composers who received South Mountain commissions and gave premieres here are legend with names like Respighi, Schoenberg, Hindemith, Saint-Saens.

In addition to the Berkshire String Quartet, now well established, guest artists have included Rudolf Serkin, the New York Pro Musica, the Waverly Consort, the Budapest, Julliard, Guarneri and Tokyo quartets, the Beaux Arts Trio and others.

The Beaux Arts has played on the mountain for 17 of the group's 23 years.

The first work ever played here was Beethoven's Opus 127 String Quartet, performed in what is still a rustic, modest, wooden building with rows of pew-like benches that seat 500.

The building itself is listed on the National Register of Historic Buildings. But locals have their own way of listing it: "A temple of music."

Tanglewood

Address: Lenox, Mass., 01240. Phone
                               413-637-1940 after June 15 for reserva-
                               tions. For earlier reservations call Sym-
                               phony Hall, Boston, 617-266-1492.
Open: June 28-August 26
Tickets: $5.50-$17.50 for the shed; $4 for lawn.
                               Rehearsals, $3.50.

Tanglewood is a 210 acre estate located between Lenox and Stockbridge.

Given to the Boston Symphony Orchestra by private bequest in 1936, it has been the permanent home of the orchestra's

Berkshire Festival ever since.

Nine weeks of concerts with famed guest conductors are given from Thursday-Sunday. Preludes 7 p.m. Friday, and concerts 8:30 p.m. Saturdays, 2:30 p.m. Sundays. A dream that all began with a group of music loving summer residents, it has come true for countless thousands ever since.

When the first musical director, Serge Koussevitzky, began a concert back in 1937 under a tent in the rain, a cry sprung up for something more substantial. A hundred thousand dollars later eminent architect Eliel Saarinen was hired to create the shed.

Tanglewood today annually draws close to a quarter of a million visitors to its concerts, weekly chamber music concerts, prelude concerts and open rehearsals. In addition, there are almost daily concerts by gifted young musicians of the Berkshire Music Center.

Arthur Fiedler and the Boston Pops perform each summer and a series of concerts by popular artists has also drawn capacity crowds.

Seiji Ozawa became Music Director of the Boston Symphony Orchestra in the fall of 1973. He is the orchestra's thirteenth conductor.

He, too, has become so enamoured with the Berkshires that he built a house in nearby West Stockbridge.

Although the sheltered shed seats for Tanglewood concerts are costly and not always easy to come by, there is always a grassy spot on the lawn where you may picnic under the stars while listening to Beethoven's Fifth, or perhaps Mozart or Dvorak.

Tanglewood has elevated picnicking to a high art, but no one here crunches, rattles or speaks above hushed tones.

Music presides at this modest or extravagant banquet table which nature sets superbly.

At intermission, or after the concert, take a moment to amble across the lawns and to enjoy the timeless beauty of the stately pines and view of Stockbridge Bowl.

Nathaniel Hawthorne enjoyed a quite similar view for about two years, 1850-1851, when he lived on what has become the Tanglewood grounds. At the time he was living in a little cottage as the guest of William Aspinwall Tappen who bought a portion of what had been Samuel Ward's estate. A replica of the cottage is now opposite the Lion Gates of Tanglewood. It was while Hawthorne lived on these grounds that he worked on "The House of Seven Gables" and began "Tanglewood Tales."

Williamstown Theatre Festival

Address: Main Street at the junction of Routes 2 and 7, Williamstown, Mass., 01267, 413-458-8146

Open: June 29 - August 27

Performances: Tuesday - Saturday evenings; matinees Thursday and Sunday

Tickets: $4 - $8.50

Adams Memorial Theater, Williamstown,
Credit: Stephanie L. Johnson

In addition to the main stage equity performances which are reason enough to come here, there are special Sunday events at the Clark Art Institute, evening cabaret performances following the theater at local night spots, and experimental inexpensive productions by the Second Company given at Pine Cobble School.

The theatre festival, which celebrates its 25th anniversary as this book is coming out, has increasingly enjoyed a national reputation for the quality of its productions and featured well known actors.

Frank Langella was loved here in numerous Chekhov plays long before Broadway toasted him as Dracula. Joel Gray and

Richard Chamberlain, Carrie Nye, Blythe Danner, Laurie Kennedy, Lee Grant, Geraldine Fitzgerald, Olympia Dukakis, have been familiar faces here. Many come back year after year like alumni at a summer reunion.

Nikos Psacharopoulos, who helped found this community theater back in 1955, became artistic director a year later and has been its cohesive force and guiding spirit ever since.

While other New England regional summer theaters waffle over their identity and ratings wane from season to season, this theater has grown in reputation and scope.

It is also a summer workshop for apprentices who compete tooth and nail for a chance to work behind the scenes creating the stuff summer theater is made of. A who's who listing of "graduates" by itself is impressive.

A highly sophisticated theater with big theatrical names and classics that run the gamut from Ibsen to Noel Coward, Moliere to Chekhov, we know it isn't just local prejudice that recommends it as the best regional summer theater.

Bousquet

Address:	South Mountain Road, off Routes 7 & 20, Pittsfield, Mass., 01201 (2 miles southwest of Pittsfield), 413-442-8808
Trails and Slopes:	750-foot drop. 14 trails and slopes: six novice, five intermediate, three expert. Eight trails lighted for night-time skiing. Longest run, 1½ miles. Snowmaking 70 percent.
Lifts:	One double-chair, two pomas, one t-bar, five rope tows
Prices:	All day lift tickets: Weekends, adults, $10; age 12 and under, $9; Weekdays, both, $6. Night: Monday and Thursday, $4; Tuesday, Wednesday, Friday and Saturday, $5.50
Instruction:	Classes for all abilities in both traditional and Head Way methods. Forty instructors. Also, racing and free style classes and February camp for youngsters.

Bousquet has been known as a teaching mountain for years. Its ski school is excellent and it has good novice and intermediate slopes. The base lodge has a cafeteria and cocktail lounge and the Racquet Club across the road has indoor tennis and handball courts as well as saunas and whirlpools to ease tired muscles.

Brodie Mountain

Address:	Route 7, New Ashford, Mass., 01237 (between Pittsfield and Williamstown), 413-443-4752
Trails and Slopes:	1,250-foot drop. 20 trails: 5 novice, 7 intermediate, 8 expert; and 3 slopes. 17 miles lighted for night time skiing. Longest run, 2½ miles. Snowmaking
Lifts:	Four double chairs, two rope tows
Prices:	All day lift tickets: weekends, adults, $13; age 14 & under, $11. Weekdays, adults, $10; age 14 & under, $9. Night: 3 - 11 p.m., $10; 7 - 11 p.m., $8
Instruction:	Downhill and cross-country

Credit: Randy Trabold

Brodie is the place to go if you're a lively single or a fun-loving couple. The apres ski activities can get as energetic as those on the slopes. Entertainment every night in the base lodge, which has a pub in the basement, a cafeteria on the main floor and a dining room upstairs that looks out over the lighted slopes. There's a motel on the grounds as well as rental and retail ski shops and a campground with electric hookups. St. Patrick's Day is a week-long celebration here.

Butternut Basin

Address:	Route 23, Great Barrington, Mass., 01230 (2 miles east of Great Barrington), 413-528-2000
Trails and Slopes:	1,000-foot drop. 11 trails. One novice, seven intermediate, three expert. Two open slopes. No night time skiing. Longest run, 7,500 feet

Lifts:	Four double-chairs, one triple-chair, one t-bar
Prices:	All day lift tickets: Weekends, adult, $13; age 13 & under, $11. Weekdays, adult, $11, age 13 & under, $10
Instruction:	Both standard and graduated length methods

Butternut Basin is family oriented and has a well-earned reputation for providing some of the best groomed and covered trails. They stockpile manmade snow to patch spots worn by skier traffic. Base lodge has a cafeteria, retail and rental shops and the nursery, for ages 3-6, is open 9 a.m. to 4 p.m. on weekends and holidays.

Catamount

Address:	Route 23, South Egremont, Mass., 01258 (7 miles from Great Barrington), 413-528-1262
Trails and Slopes:	1,000 foot drop. 23 trails. Nine novice, nine intermediate, five expert. Longest run, 2 miles. Snowmaking 14 of 23 areas
Lifts:	Three double-chairs, two t-bars, one j-bar
Prices:	All day lift ticket: weekends, adults, $13; age 10 & under, $10. Weekdays, adults, $10; age 10 & under, $9. Night: Tuesday, Wednesday and Friday, 4:30 - 10 p.m., adults $7; children, $5
Instruction:	American and graduated length methods. 40 instructors. Videotape lessons. Racing and freestyle classes for youngsters and beginners classes for tots

Catamount is a lovely, scenic ski area straddling the Massachusetts, New York border. The recently enlarged base lodge has rental and retail shops and a cafeteria and dining room with beamed ceiling and windows overlooking the mountain.

In summer, a mile-long mountain coaster operates 10 a.m. to dusk, daily between July 1 and Sept. 4; weekends only from May

27 to June 30 and Sept. 5 to mid October. Tickets are $2.75 per ride for adults, $1.75 for ages 7-12, and free for children under 6 accompanied by adult.

Jiminy Peak

Address: Corey Road, off Route 7, or Route 43, Hancock, Mass., 01237 (14 miles northwest of Pittsfield, 20 miles from Williamstown, 413-738-5431

Trails and
Slopes: 1,143-foot drop. 25 trails and slopes, novice to expert. Longest run 2 miles. Snowmaking 70 percent of area

Lifts: Four double-chairs, one rope tow

Prices: All day lift ticket: weekends, adults, $13; age 12 & under, $10. Weekdays, adults and children, $9. Night: Monday - Saturday, 3-10:30 p.m., $8; 6-10:30 p.m., $7

Instruction: Yes

There's a dignity and refinement about Jiminy that most big ski areas lack. Many consider it the most challenging mountain in the Berkshires. The base lodge has a cafeteria and rental shop and a supervised playroom.

During the summer, a 2,890-foot alpine slide operates daily from 10 a.m. to dusk, July 1-Sept. 4; and on weekends and holidays from May 6-June 24 and Sept. 9 to Oct. 29. Tickets are $2.50 per ride for adults; $1.50 for children. Under 6, free, accompanied by parent.

Otis Ridge

Address: Route 8, Otis, Mass., 01253 413-269-4444

Trails and
Slopes: 375-foot drop. Eight trails and six slopes, novice to expert. No night skiing. Longest run 3,800 feet. Snowmaking 80 percent of area

Lifts: One poma lift, one t-bar, one j-bar, three rope tows

Prices: All day lift tickets: weekends, adults, $8.50; children, $7.50. Weekdays, adults, $6; children, $4.50

Instruction: Junior ski camp for youngsters 8 to 16 is one of the largest in the northeast. Classes on weekends and school vacations combine skiing with other winter sports

Otis Ridge is a small, friendly mountain that lies in a snow belt and, with snowmaking to help, often provides good skiing when other areas are having problems.

Base lodge has a canteen, rental and retail shops.

SKIING: NORDIC

Beartown State Forest
Great Barrington and Monterey, Mass., off Route 23.

Ten miles of cross-country ski trails as well as miles of old logging roads and hiking trails. Parking near the headquarters building, Route 23, Monterey. Trail maps available at the office.

Bartholomew's Cobble
Weateague Road, Sheffield, Mass.

A natural area managed by the Massachusetts Trustees of Reservations, Bartholomew's Cobble has several miles of hiking trails through open fields along the banks of the Housatonic River. The trail to Hurlburt Hill may tempt the more experienced.

Canoe Meadows
Holmes Road, Pittsfield, Mass.

A wildlife sanctuary with seven miles of forest and farmland trails and a 40-acre open field for beginners. Parking area at 350 Williams Street.

Cluett Hill - Stone Hill
South Street, Williamstown, Mass.

Both of these trails start near the Clark Art Institute. Cluett, the easier of the two and about three miles long, starts behind the Clark and follows an old road across pastureland. Stone Hill begins at the entrance to the Buxton School and makes a loop about two miles long through hilly forest — a challenge to intermediate skiers. Beginners may also want to try the Williams College golf course across the street from the Clark with its rolling greens and beautiful mountain views. No trail fees or rental.

Brodie Mountain
Route 7, New Ashford, Mass., 01237, 413-443-4752

Ten miles of groomed trails operated in conjunction with the Brodie Mountain downhill ski area. Lodge is open to cross country skiers. Trail fee: all day, $3; after 1 p.m., $2. Rentals: all day, $5; after 1 p.m., $4. Private and group instruction available.

Butternut Basin
Route 23, Great Barrington, Mass., 01230, 413-528-2000

Ski touring center operated independent of the downhill facility has novice and intermediate trails that loop around a pond and meadow. Instruction offered between 10 a.m. and 2 p.m.

Winter's solitude, Credit: Randy Trabold

Egremont Country Club
South Egremont, Mass., 01258, 413-528-4222

250 acres of open field, golf course and woodland trail, one lighted at night. Trail fee: Adults, $2, under 12, $1. Free to renters. Rentals: weekends, $7 (after 1 p.m. $5); weekdays, $5. Refreshments and box lunches at clubhouse.

Eugene D. Moran Wildlife Center
Route 8A, Windsor, Mass.

1,000 acres abutting Windsor State Forest, mostly open land with fine views.

The Center at Foxhollow
Route 7, Lenox, Mass., 01240, 413-637-2000

Ten miles of groomed trails around a former estate. Trail fee, $2. Rentals and instruction. Refreshments at the inn.

Jug End Resort
Routes 23 and 41, South Egremont, Mass., 01258, 413-528-0434

1,200 acre resort with open fields, golf course and miles of groomed trails. Box lunches available. Trail fee: $1.50 per day. Rentals: $7.50 per day. Group instruction: $5.

Notchview Reservation
Route 9, Windsor, Mass.

25 miles of trails through 3,000 acres of forest and open meadow owned by the Massachusetts Trustees of Reservations. Waxing and warming room in the headquarters building where trail maps are available.

Pittsfield State Forest
West Street, Pittsfield, Mass.

A heavily used ski touring area with many well-marked trails for all levels of ability. Maps available at the park headquarters. Snowmobiling allowed and weekends can get busy.

Pleasant Valley Wildlife Sanctuary
Route 7, Lenox, Mass.

A nature area maintained by the Massachusetts Audubon Society with 14 miles of trails, mostly for beginners. Parking and trail maps at the headquarters building which also has a waxing and warming room. Admission: 50 cents to non Audubon members.

Kennedy Park
Lenox, Mass.

A town-owned park with 13 miles of marked trails from beginning to expert. Site of the former Aspinwall Hotel which burned in 1931. You can still see the ruins. Trail maps available at the Chamber of Commerce. Parking at the Church-on-the-Hill.

Oak 'n Spruce
South Lee, Mass., 01260, 413-243-3500

Golf course and woodland trails that connect to Beartown State Forest. Open only on weekends. Trail fee: $2 per day. Rentals: $8. No instruction.

Lost Wilderness Ski Touring Center
Sandisfield, Mass., 01255, 413-258-4872.

25 miles of trails, some groomed. Lodge has snacks and meals. Trail fee: $1; free to rentals. Rentals; $7 per day; $5.25 after 12 noon. Instruction: private and group.

Otis Ridge Ski Touring Center
Route 23, Otis; Mass., 01253, 413-269-4444

Practice meadow for beginners and two one-mile trails leading to 15 miles of trails in Otis State Forest. Cafeteria at base lodge of downhill facility. No trail fee. Rentals: $6 per day; $4 after 1 p.m. Instruction: $5 group lesson.

Savoy State Forest
Central Shaft Road, south of Route 2, Savoy, Mass.

Some say this is among the best ski-touring areas in the Berkshires. Williams College cross-country team trains here. 12 miles of trails, some groomed, for all abilities, with a circular practice track. Park at the North Pond lot. Maps available at park headquarters.

Taconic Crest Trail
29-mile trail from the Vermont line through Pittsfield State Forest to Route 20 in New Lebanon, N.Y. Easy access at Petersburg Pass on Route 43 Williamstown, near Mt. Raimer Ski area. Mostly for intermediate to expert. Trail guide and information available free from the Taconic Hiking Club by writing to Raymond H. Johnston, 50 Neward St., Cohoes, N.Y. 12047. The Williams College Outing Club also published a guide which may be purchased at Williamstown bookstores.

Golf, tennis, swimming, boating, horseback riding, canoeing, are so readily available and numerous that we aren't attempting a selective list. The best swimming holes are closely guarded secrets. No one wants a thousand people to know at once, but, if you ask, your innkeeper will tell YOU.

For the best list of state forests and parks as well as individual area maps write: Massachusetts Department of Environmental Management, Division of Forests and Parks, 100 Cambridge Street, Boston, Mass. 02202. It is free.

If you want to hike trails in these woods, get a copy of the Appalachian Trail Guide and start picking from the 83.8 miles of the Massachusetts portion. The Williams (College) Outing Club book will also tell you what you need to know about local trails, distances and sites.

There are 10 open-to-the-public 18-and 9-hole golf courses located from South Egremont to Williamstown, one bound to be within a 20 minute drive from wherever you may be.

Tennis, indoor or out, all year round, is very often readily available at local high schools and town parks as well as by reservation at private resorts and clubs.

If you want to get onto the water, you can launch anything that floats free at Stockbridge Bowl, Stockbridge; Onota Lake, Pittsfield; and Hoosac Lake, Cheshire. The largest selection of rentals, everything from rowboats and canoes to motorboats and various small sailing craft, is at Pontoosuc Lake, Route 7, Pittsfield. Rentals are also available at Greenwater Pond, Becket; Hoosac Lake, Cheshire; Goose Pond, Lee; Laurel Lake, Lee; Prospect Lake, North Egremont; Otis Reservoir, Otis; and Richmond Pond, Richmond.

If perchance you're still in a quandry wondering what else to do, we suggest:

— A visit to the **Berkshire Garden Center**, Routes 102 and 183 west of Stockbridge where beautiful gardens, lily ponds, herbs, youth programs, exhibits, lectures, workshops and a gift shop await you.

— A jaunt to the **Otis Poultry Farm**, Route 8, North Otis, open daily 8 a.m.-6 p.m. Friday to Sunday to sample homemade chicken and turkey pies, fruit pies, breads, cakes, jams and jellies, fresh cider, maple syrup and honey and homemade peanut butter. A good place to select your Thanksgiving Tom turkey or stock up on a dozen fresh laid eggs.

Pontoosuc Lake, Pittsfield, Credit: Stephanie L. Johnson

A visit to **Caretaker Farm**, Hancock Road, Williamstown, where they pride themselves on organically grown produce on 35 lovingly tended acres and annually turn out the largest heads of lettuce we've ever seen. It is open to the public 9 a.m.-6 p.m. daily and part of the fun is asking Elizabeth and Sam Smith all about it.

—A trip to the **Berkshire Fish Hatchery**, Monterey, one of the U.S. Department of Interior hatcheries that specializes in raising Atlantic salmon to replenish the Connecticut River and its tributaries. Open every day, weekends and holidays 8 a.m.-4:30 p.m., it has resident ecologists who will tell you how a salmon goes from a tiny egg to a large fish capable of swimming to Greenland and back to spawn. It's fascinating.

—Drive up the Mohawk Trail in North Adams toward Whitcomb Summit and take the first left before the top, Moore's Road. Follow the signs to **Bear Meadow Farm** where 150 varieties of herbs are grown by Barbara and Reuben Shay. They are for sale, in pots to go, dried, in jams, vinegars, jellies and breads that you'll wish you had a dozen of. Open to the public 9:30 a.m. to 4:30 p.m. every day but Tuesday. Mrs. Shay is a walking herbal encyclopedia.

—Stand under the **Children's Chime Tower** in Stockbridge and listen to the chimes for a half-hour each evening during

June, July and August. A variety of popular tunes are played between 5:30 p.m. and 6 p.m. each evening. The century old Children's Chime Tower was donated in 1878 by New Yorker David Dudley Field in the name of his grandchildren living and dead. The tower marks the spot where the Little Church in the Wilderness once stood when John Sergeant preached to the Stockbridge Indians in 1739.

— If nothing on earth has thus moved you, head to the **Milham Planetarium** located in the Old Hopkins Observatory building on the Williams College campus. It sits on a small hill on the south side of Main Street (Route 2) in Williamstown between Spring and Water Streets. There is a small museum of astronomy here, very often interesting astronomy programs, and telescopic sky watching, weather permitting. Open every Tuesday and Thursday evening, June 15-August 10, 8 p.m. No admission charge, but a phone-in reservation is recommended because it is small. 423-597-2188.

— Tired of waiting for local movies to change? Go to **Images Cinema** on Spring Street, Williamstown, where new flicks, foreign goodies and classics are served up every two or three days year round. **Toad Hall**, at Music Inn, Lenox, has a similar interesting and changeable celluloid diet, but it serves only in summer. In winter they close up and hibernate in Greenwich Village, New York. Both places usually roll their reels at two showings, at 7 and 9 p.m. Or, if you're farther south, head to the **Mahaiwe Theatre**, Railroad Street, Great Barrington, and see what's playing at this old theater; it varies.

— Looking for a zoo? Try **Springside Park** in Pittsfield, a children's zoo open 10 a.m. to dusk, mid April to October. There are exhibits of barnyard animals, occasional talks and weekend demonstrations.

— Rent a bike and explore Berkshire backroads. **Moped Rentals,** Route 183 between Lenox and Tanglewood, open daily 9 a.m.-6 p.m., is in the heart of the best biking territory.

FOOD

The Cornucopian Natural Foods Store, 424 North Street, Pittsfield, is what its name implies, a horn of plenty for health food lovers. But if your appetite doesn't perk up with rabbit food, that's not all that is here. Take out lunches are delicious. Syrian bread stuffed with bean sprouts, fresh tomatoes, tofu, olives, $1. Fresh juices squeezed while you wait. And try the fresh banana ice cream made in the blender while you wait at 25 cents a scoop.

Samel's Deli Shop, 115 Elm Street, Pittsfield, looks just like a grocery store, but the sandwich menu rivals the best New York deli and you can sit down and nosh away. Salads, sandwiches, bagels, cheese, Haagen Daaz ice cream, Perrier water, crackers and cookies. A good place to fill up a picnic basket for Tanglewood.

Diau's Deli, Spring Street, Williamstown, has some of the fattest and most whimsically named deli sandwiches concocted. Fresh blended juices, yogurt shakes, exotic fruit drinks, local mineral water on tap and bottled, imported cheeses, salads, and Fairdale Farms fresh farm ice cream are found here.

Slippery Banana, Spring Street, Williamstown, has barrels of nuts, dried fruits, fresh vegetables, assorted teas and coffee ground to order.

The Cheese and Sausage Shop, Pittsfield-Lenox Road, Routes 7 and 20, Lenox, will pack you a Tanglewood picnic basket to go. Just phone ahead for jumbo deli sandwiches, various cheeses.

Locke Stock & Barrel, Stockbridge Road, Great Barrington, has a mind boggling array of fascinating natural foods. There are 15 kinds of honey plus Chinese food ingredients, cheeses and crackers.

There are other bakers, but there is only one **Suchele Bakers,** 31 Housatonic Street, Lenox. This teeny place gets our recommendation hands down as the best baker in Berkshire County, a pastry paradise. There are chocolate filled croissants, cream filled hazelnut Danishes, and always fresh baked breads of every ingredient popping out of the in-sight oven.

Catherine's Chocolate Shoppe, Stockbridge Road, Great Barrington, has been making hand-dipped confections for a long, long time. A lot of Catherine's made in the kitchen bite sized miniatures make up a pound bag.

ARTS AND CRAFTS

Not surprisingly, art galleries have begun to sprout up like field flowers.

We don't know which came first, but **Clemens Kalischer's Images Gallery** has been in the Mews in Stockbridge since this internationally known photographer first moved here from New York City in 1965. Fearing a flood of tourists during the

Bicentennial he temporarily locked his doors and the serious browsers rang the bell.

Not yet as well known, and happily less harried, are a dozen other small galleries scattered throughout the county.

Worth a look in north county is **The Gallery**, 85 Spring Street, Williamstown, which features contemporary graphics, paintings, sculpture and some hand crafted items mostly created by local artists who are gaining respected reputations.

Really a craft shop, but of such consistent fine quality and artful display that we are placing it in this list is **The Potter's Wheel**, Water Street, Williamstown, where you will find pottery, the works of glass sculptors and blowers, and weavers and jewelry craftsmen.

In North Adams, the Northern Berkshire Council of the Arts exhibits crafts by area artists at **The Corner**, inside the Sheraton Inn, 40 Main Street.

Down in Lenox the **Yamato Gallery**, 104 Main Street, is a Japanese tea party of beautiful Japanese prints, ceramics, and contemporary works. Over at the **Honey Sharp Gallery**, 90 Church Street, next door to the Ganesh Cafe, you will find a bright and informal gallery where works of internationally known artists as well as Berkshire artists are shown.

In Lee, at **J. and J. Lubrano**, on Route 102, there is a unique collection of musical materials, prints, instruments, rare books and music.

Tiny Tyringham, an off the beaten path village still unspoiled and once favored by the likes of Twain and naturalist John Burroughs, boasts the most unusual gallery, aptly named **The Gingerbread House.** Formerly the studio of sculptor Sir Henry Hudson Kitson who created the Minute Man at Lexington, and now a contemporary art gallery, this building is really a piece in itself. The roof is rolling fastened by two tons of nails in a manner that gives it a witch-like visage. The works inside are mostly modern American.

Down in Sheffield, the heart of Berkshire county antique country, just north of the Connecticut border on Route 7, is the **Westenhook Gallery** which has etchings, serigraphs, paintings, photographs and sculpture, mostly contemporary.

There are other galleries scattered and continually sprouting up in Stockbridge, West Stockbridge, Lenox, Lee and Great Barrington.

CLOTHING

In north county, **The House of Walsh**, Spring Street, Williamstown, has put fine threads on the backs of young and old Williams College students for years. Need we say more? There's also a women's shop.

Roberta's, State Road, Route 2, Williamstown, is a nest of fine sportswear separates, a veritable Beene bag.

In central Berkshire, downtown Pittsfield, the **1886 Shop**, 26 Bank Row, and **Brothership Clothing** at 141 North Street, have fine suits, separates and sportswear. Both have women's shops. **Beba,** the sister shop to Brothership, has a selection that will appeal to Gucci-look lovers.

In south county, **Talbots,** 46 Walker Street, Lenox, and **Elise Farar,** 361 Pittsfield Road, have an envied corner on women's country classic sportswear, sherbet colored monogramed sweaters and designer labels. Also check out **The Lemon Tree**, Main Street, Lenox, a sweet find for clothing as well as house and hostess gifts.

England's, 89 North Street, Pittsfield, is Berkshire County's oldest and largest fine department store.

Cottage II, 63 Water Street, Williamstown, and **Cottage IV**, 31 South Street, Pittsfield, are one of the youngest, most colorful market places for clothing, gifts and unusual decorative items for the home.

For oldies, but goodies, our favorite second hand vintage collections are found at **Down Home**, 173 Main Street, Great Barrington, and **Yesterday's General Store**, in Lanesboro, Route 7. The clothing here is clean as a whistle and some frocks are whistle stop material.

Outdoorsmen and women who are true back packers, as well as those who just like a quality look and wear, will find what they need at **Arcadian Shops,** in north county at 1 Water Street, Williamstown, in south county at 44 Housatonic Street, Lenox. They also rent cross country skis in winter.

South of Great Barrington, across the town line in Sheffield, is another outdoor person's favorite haunt. **Riverrun North** has clothing and rents skis in winter, canoes in summer.

Kenver Ltd., Route 23, Egremont, in a rambling 230 year old former tavern in a quiet and quaint country village, has probably just about every ski you could take off on, plus a wide selection of summertime tennis togs.

The most amazing antique, curio, bric-a-brac shop in the county has to be **Joneses'**. Located off Route 7, opposite the Great Barrington Fairgrounds, there are five full acres and four buildings crammed, jammed with everything... including the kitchen sink. It is a three ring circus for pokers, a bargain hunter's happy hunting ground.

Jenifer House, Route 7, Great Barrington, is the region's "Americana," gift shop. Everything from furniture to fine china and penny candies are found here. Soap dishes from merry old England, glass of every description, and gifts galore. How they ever manage an inventory is a task we don't care to imagine.

Old book bugs would do well to head to **Second Life Book Shop**, Upper East Hoosac Street, Adams, where they will find a barn with 20,000 works classified by subject. Also **The Carriage Barn**, Cold Spring Road, Route 7, next to Elwal Pines Motel, Williamstown, where a carriage house has been converted to provide a cozy atmosphere for browsing. There are at least 15,000 books for the casual or serious browser, organized by area of interest, especially Americana.

Looking for a lot of antiques under one roof? Head to **Twin Fires Arcade,** the junction of Under Mountain Road, Route 41, and Berkshire School Road, Sheffield, where a recreated arcade and stall of shops such as you would expect of England in the mid 1800's has been fashioned. The refurbished barn contains fine early American as well as Victorian, Georgian and early Welsh pieces. Also, lots of unfinished pine. Getting here is almost half the fun since you will pass countless antique and curio shops all through Sheffield which is an antiquarian's attic for fine finds. Other fine antique shops scattered about the county are listed in the Berkshire Antique Dealer's free pamphlet. Just ask at any town information booth.